LAW'S
STRANGEST®
CASES

Other titles in the STRANGEST series

LAW'S STRANGEST® CASES

Extraordinary but true stories
from over five centuries of legal history

PETER SEDDON

PORTICO

Published in the United Kingdom in 2016 by
Portico
1 Gower Street
London
WC1E 6HD

An imprint of Pavilion Books Company Ltd

ISBN 978-1-91023-289-7

A CIP catalogue record for this book is available from the British Library.

10 9 8 7 6 5 4 3 2 1

Reproduction by Colourdepth UK
Printed and bound by Bookwell, Finland

This book can be ordered direct from the publisher at www.pavilionbooks.com

CONTENTS

'How often have I said to you that when you have eliminated the impossible, whatever remains, however improbable, must be the truth?'

Sherlock Holmes, *The Sign of the Four* (1890)

INTRODUCTION

Few laymen would claim to be fascinated by accountancy or banking, despite their undoubted entertainment potential. Yet legal matters are altogether different, for equally few laymen would claim not to be seduced by the stories of murder, intrigue, crime, punishment and the pursuit of justice that have made 'The Law' such a perennially popular subject, more on a par with sport and the entertainment industry than its close relations in other professions. With that in mind I put it to you that the law is 'theatre' – with a cast of thousands, a multitude of heroes and villains, improvised scripts and cliffhanger endings never revealed until the very last second of the final act.

It is for reasons of entertainment, therefore, that I offer the curious accounts in *The Law's Strangest Cases*, a collection of true stories that illustrate the idiosyncrasies of legal (and illegal) doings throughout centuries of history.

The choice at my disposal was mind-boggling. The easiest methodology would have been to fill the book with celebrated murder trials, but I opted instead to track down a much broader range of cases that would illustrate the many different facets of the law and the larger-than-life characters who seek either to make it or break it.

The result is a purely personal selection in which humour, oddity and the macabre loom large. There are medieval tales such as the mass trial of moles for vandalism ('The Accused

Have Gone to Ground') and the most outlandish admission of guilt of all time ('An Imaginative Confession'). There are astonishing survivals of the death penalty ('Well, I'll Be Hanged!'), the 'corpse' who gave spoken evidence at his own inquest ('The Eleventh Witness') and the heartening story of Capstick, the most diligent police officer of all time.

Murder inevitably rears its ugly but strangely irresistible head in a number of my selections. 'Trust Me, I'm a Doctor' would be too far-fetched even for Victorian melodrama, yet thanks to Harold Shipman, the doctor with the worst bedside manner of all time, that all-too-true account comes towards the end of the book at the dawn of the 'civilised' twenty-first century.

Other murder cases display a more light-hearted touch. Consider the murderess who collected rent from her mummified victim for 21 years ('A Very Quiet Tenant') or the wishful thinker who gave himself away by describing himself in a job application as 'a widower' *before* he'd bumped off his wife ('A Man Ahead of His Time').

I imagined that judges might add a sober balance to such ridiculous tales as the serial cutlery-swallower ('A Knife-and-Fork Job') but how wrong I was, for time and again they simply demanded inclusion for reasons every bit as bizarre. I could no more leave out the English judge whose penchant for whisky and cigarettes landed him with a smuggling conviction ('One Case Too Many') than I could the Welsh judge who had his wig stolen in court ('A Symbolic Crime'). Barristers too have had their moments. None more so than the exasperated American who appealed for a verdict to be reversed because the opposition had broken wind throughout his closing speech ('The Most Desperate Appeal Ever').

Even animals get a look-in. 'Not So Dumb Witness' recalls Tetter the dog, who gave winning evidence at an industrial tribunal, and the most famous snail in legal history is honoured in the celebrated 1920s case which blazed a trail to the compensation culture we know today ('Once Pickled, Forever Toasted').

The bulk of the cases are from Britain, with the Old Bailey figuring prominently, but I found it impossible to exclude a number from the United States and elsewhere, as strangeness is as likely to strike in Sydney and New York, or at the nether regions of Carlisle and Colchester, as at the very heart of the English legal system itself.

My sources were many and I am particularly indebted to the anonymous scribes who compiled *The All England Law Reports* and the many accomplished more 'popular' writers whose published works alerted me to cases I might have otherwise overlooked.

Although I studied law as a module at university, I did not enter the profession. I have approached the subject as an experienced practitioner of 'strangeology', but through the eyes of a legal layman. So *The Law's Strangest Cases* is no dry legal textbook, but rather a sideways look at the subject from a light-hearted standpoint, although with serious overtones never far away.

I would like to thank friends and members of the legal profession for suggesting subject matter, and my editors Nicola Newman and Katie Hewett for bringing the book to fruition. Let proceedings commence.

Peter Seddon

THE STRANGEST CASE
OF ALL TIME?

JERUSALEM, c.AD 33

The accused apparently died at 3p.m. on Friday, 3 April, AD 33, although strangely some say it was three years earlier. Others assert that he didn't die at all. The records are inconclusive. The method of execution was barbaric and there had been no proper trial, only a hastily convened mock court presided over by officials of varying degrees of corruption. That 'trial', moreover, was conducted under Jewish law within which the empowerment to pass a death sentence was questionable. The Jewish authorities overcame this trifling difficulty by trumping up suitably embellished charges and handing the prisoner over to the Roman authorities, who operated under a completely different legal code by which powers of execution were unlimited.

Yet the Roman Governor of Judea was sceptical of the charges against his newly delivered prisoner. Yes, he had entered Jerusalem during the week preceding the great festival of Passover. Yes, he had aroused great fervour among many of the 300,000 pilgrims gathered in the city. Yes, he had preached at the temple and overturned the stalls of merchants trying to conduct business around it. He was a dissident of sorts, it was true. Perhaps even a prophet, as his disciples were to claim. But was he really 'King of the Jews', a direct threat to Roman authority? And was he truly 'the son of God' or just a harmless traveller with ideas beyond his station, skilled at making capital from a gullible public?

The Roman Governor was tempted to release his charge, for it was his custom to grant freedom to one prisoner during the Passover festivities. He was, too, rather afraid of the reaction of the prisoner's followers if the death sentence was confirmed. He decided to pursue a novel judicial procedure, putting the vote to the gathered crowd of Jews.

He announced to the unruly throng that he found no fault with the man in his custody; but, despite his charismatic appeal in some quarters, the prisoner got the thumbs-down from the majority and was therefore sent to execution on nothing more than a public show of hands. To compound the treachery of this flagrant miscarriage of justice, another prisoner, Barabbas, a known murderer, was freed instead.

Before his execution the condemned man was humiliated, verbally taunted and beaten by guards. And, after being subjected to that brutality at the hands of authority, he was forced to walk at daybreak, heavily burdened, to the place of execution, where he was nailed to a wooden cross. It took six lingering hours for the death by crucifixion to run its course.

We might add other curious oddities to this astonishing account. For starters, the condemned man had been betrayed by a 'supergrass' who was one of his own gang. And, by way of further sensationalism, some reports confirmed that the crucified man, after he had been taken from the cross by his friends, came back to life three days later.

It is the sort of story with which twenty-first-century tabloid newspapers would have a field day. Was Pontius Pilate, the Roman Governor of Judea, really the villain of the piece? Or did that dubious honour fall to the Jewish high priest, Caiaphas, head of the 'kangaroo court' that contrived the prisoner's demise? Could someone dish the dirt on Barabbas the reprieved murderer? We need an exclusive interview with the 'grass' Judas Iscariot – headline the piece THE KISS OF DEATH and offer him 30 shekels. Has anyone tracked down the 'dead' man Jesus of Nazareth? Is he really still alive, or was it the 'resurrection men', the body snatchers, who left the rock-cut tomb devoid of a corpse? There have been reported sightings, but could there be an impostor on the loose? Just get that story!

All these questions and many more related to the case have assailed the troubled minds of every generation for nearly 2,000 years. Yet the accounts of the events in Jerusalem are tantalisingly at odds with each other. Even those written a few decades later based on eyewitness evidence offer disparate solutions. Should we believe St Luke or should we favour other chroniclers of the biblical age? What, after all, really is the Gospel truth?

Scholars have argued the case since time immemorial. Bitter wars have been fought over the principles involved. Followers of the Christian religion believe passionately that the accused was cruelly wronged and that he did rise again. Sceptics say it's all a load of bunkum, just a heavily embroidered folk tapestry with far too many loose ends showing.

The Temple Authorities v. Jesus of Nazareth is arguably the strangest legal case of all time, so enshrouded in mystique that the whole truth seems likely to remain undiscovered for eternity. As we go to press the jury is still out and seems set to deliberate for some time.

LADY MARION'S ORDEAL
HEREFORD ASSIZES, 1207

But for the legacy of King Alfred the Great (849–99), the ardent Lady Marion of Hereford might have been able to indulge in a spot of hanky-panky without getting her fingers burnt. As it was, she was caught red-handed.

That Alfred burnt the cakes may merely be the stuff of legend. Of greater certainty was the tireless effort of this most celebrated of Saxon kings in bringing a degree of much-needed unity to the disparate Saxon kingdoms he presided over when he became King of Wessex in 871.

And nowhere was his intelligent approach more influential than in the field of English law. No sooner had the 22-year-old taken the throne than his *Book of Laws* made its appearance, combining the best long-held but primitive legal customs of Kent and Mercia with those of Wessex, throwing in some good solid biblical guidelines for good measure and adding a hint of Germanic and Roman legislation to the eclectic mix.

The resulting Saxon Law, which was still going strong over 300 years later, was by no means the complex and much-lauded English legal system that came to be a watchword for 'justice' the world over, but it was a start, and Alfred's advice in what was known as his Golden Rule sounds pretty sensible over a millennium later: 'What ye will that other men should not do to you, do ye not to other men.'

It may be a basic reworking of a more famous biblical guideline, but if Alfred's good citizens had followed his advice then all sorts of dastardly deeds might never have got beyond the cunning plan stage.

Alas 'boys will be boys' and a system of compensatory fines or atonements proved necessary to help control the behaviour of a populace that seemingly couldn't help itself. Killed any common labourers lately? A 200-shilling fine was sure to follow. What about poking out a serf's eye? A mere 50 shillings. And anyone prepared to cough up 3,600 shillings could really go for broke and bump off an archbishop (or 18 labourers). Then there was adultery, which in Lady Marion's case seems to have been of the multiple variety. Combining it with murder wasn't a good idea, and the Hereford Assizes court papers for 1207 record that she was accused of 'procuring her husband's murder, because she had committed adultery with a great many men, and after his death all his goods went missing from the house'.

A number of Marion's suspected lovers fled the area once the hue and cry started, and things didn't look good for the lady whose rampant sexual appetite was about to give her a spot of bother.

'What an ordeal!' How many times do we hear that throwaway line these days? But in Saxon times the phrase had an all too real ring to it, for trial by ordeal was a standard way of establishing guilt or innocence in the days before trial by jury became the norm. Ordeal was the Saxons' way of 'letting God decide', the *judicium Dei*. There were a number of options of varying unpleasantness and Lady Marion was duly called upon to face ordeal by iron.

Naturally enough the 'court' was a church. Present would be a sheriff of the shire, representing the peacekeeping force of the land, and a bishop, representing the celestial judge on high. The trial took place during Mass but the large chalice of hot coals burning near the altar wasn't to warm the congregation.

A rod of iron was thrust into the fire, made red hot and planted firmly into Lady Marion's outstretched hand. Three marks had been made on the floor and the accused was ordered to walk a distance of nine paces, which she was allowed to complete in three large strides before dropping the iron and stumbling to the altar, probably screaming, to be bandaged. Part two of the trial took place three days later, when the parties reassembled for the ceremonious removal of the bandages. If the hand was cleanly healing the culprit was pronounced innocent by a cry of 'God be praised!' If it proved to be uncleanly festering then guilt was the verdict.

A variation on the theme was the ordeal by hot water, in which the hand was plunged into a boiling vat to retrieve a ring or coin. On other occasions the hands were spared and walking the distance on hot ploughshares was implemented instead. By comparison, the ordeal by cold water, reserved for the lowly, was a doddle. In this the accused was bound and suspended from a rope, then lowered gently into the village pond. The idea was that God accepted the innocent fully into the waters, so incongruously it was the sinkers who were pardoned and the floaters who were guilty.

As for Lady Marion, the records state merely that she was 'given the iron' so her fate must be presumed, but whatever the outcome she would have been well advised to control her amorous instincts.

At least for the next 12 years, that is, for trial by ordeal was abolished by Henry III in 1219. Maybe he had sympathies in the illicit-dalliance camp. Or more likely his advisers did. Henry was only 12 at the time, surely too young even for Lady Marion.

A CHAMPION'S
UNSEEMLY END
TYNEMOUTH PRIORY, 1220

The ancient practice of trial by battle (see 'So Whose Ox
is it, Anyway?) was all very well if the parties were sound
in body and mind but not awfully effective in the case of
weaklings, cowards or the mentally feeble.

Priests and the rich were particularly noted for shying away
from judgment by fisticuffs, and therein lies the origin of
the practice of hiring a 'champion' to fight their battles for
them. Champions with good track records were naturally
keenly sought.

One such was William Pygun, a monk at St Albans known
to provide a half-decent service to the spiritually inclined, a
sort of 'Champions-U-Like' for the monastery community
of the Middle Ages.

But alas, even champions have to lose sometimes, and the
wretched William Pygun met his end in most unusual and
undignified circumstances.

Pygun was no ordinary monk. Medieval monasteries
provided sanctuary for all sorts of villains and he was
described by a contemporary chronicler as 'not so much
a monk as a twisting fiend'. An odious fellow and therefore
an ideal champion. But his luck started to run out when
he was caught forging land deeds and using the St Albans
Abbey seal to authenticate them. His punishment was
a severe one, not quite as bad as breaking on the wheel,
being buried alive, sawn in half or impaled on a stake, but

pretty horrific all the same. Pygun was put on the transfer list and sent north to Tynemouth Priory. It was farewell to the Arcadian delights of St Albans. Gone were the carefree walks through verdant meadows. And those lazy afternoons in the hazy calm of the Abbey herb garden were but a distant memory. In their place were dank draughty corridors, vermin-infested dormitories and severe northeast weather, for Tynemouth was non-league in the monastery standings. Pygun was soon pressed into action as champion to the prior in a monetary dispute with one Simon of Tynemouth, but his boxing skills deserted him. He survived the trial by battle, but was deemed the loser and shunned by his fellow monks. He turned not to God for solace but to drink and overindulgence.

His sorry end swiftly followed and was later chronicled in the *Deeds of the Abbots of St Albans:*

It happened one night that William was sitting on the lavatory and he forgot the early service and went on sitting there, drunk and bloated after gorging himself. He began to sleep and his snores were loud and disgusting and soon that sleep turned into death which may have been from the cold but more likely the vengeance of God, for when the snoring stopped a voice from the privy was clearly heard bellowing 'Get him, Satan, get him' and in this disgraceful way this wretch lost his life whilst using the lavatory.

Many men have suffered extended lavatorial trials after a night of overindulgence (the torture following nine pints of real ale and a vindaloo is known to be particularly severe) but only William Pygun has been tried in such buttock-clenching circumstances.

The monks reluctantly granted Pygun a Christian burial without due ceremony. The story of his undignified trial and death sentence in mid-bowel-evacuation mode is perfectly true. But that attaching to his appropriate epitaph is purely apocryphal: 'Taken at the Almighty's convenience. So much still to do'.

SO WHOSE OX IS IT, ANYWAY?

CARLISLE, 1292

'I am not guilty and this I am ready to defend with my body.' The likelihood of such a staunch defence being offered today, except as pure bravado, is slim indeed. Doubtless individuals still meet occasionally on a darkened night to thrash out some private grievance with the gloves off, but there is no part in the modern legal system for such barbarous ways of delivering justice.

Not so in the Middle Ages, when the so-called trial by battle was all the rage. Indeed, having a rage was quite useful if the suspect threw down the gauntlet to his accusers. Believing passionately in one's innocence was as good a way to get one's dander up as any.

It was the battling Normans who popularised the practice in England after a little skirmish on Senlac Hill, near Hastings, on 14 October 1066. On that occasion, as every school pupil used to know, William, Duke of Normandy, put one over on Harold II, King of England, to become King William I, 'the Conqueror'. Harold lost both an eye and his life during the confrontation on the field now adjacent the East Sussex town of Battle.

The Normans carried this penchant for battling into the legal system by formalising combat into a means of deciding guilt or innocence. Like trial by ordeal, it was seen as a religious rite, and the accused swore on the Bible that he was not guilty of the offence before submitting the decision to the will of God. Men were prepared to risk their lives over what seem in retrospect to be trivial offences, but, as the punishment for being found guilty might be losing a foot or a hand, having an eye gouged out or being put to death by a variety of horrific means, many were prepared to take a chance.

Hugh Bolare was one such. Having just acquired a new ox, he wasn't averse to cruising around with it in a rather ostentatious fashion so that the neighbours got the message. No doubt he gave it a wash-down every Sunday morning. This seems to have got up the nose of one 'Gilbert the Goose', who accused the boastful Hugh of stealing it from him at the court of Robert le Brus. 'Leave it out,' quoth Hugh – or in medieval words to that effect – much put out by Gilbert's bare-faced cheek: 'I bought the ox honestly from William the Long.'

Perhaps it's best not to conjecture how said Willie got his name, but suffice to say he created a major impasse by denying the ox had ever been his.

There was nothing for it but trial by battle, so at Carlisle in 1292, the court ordered that Hugh should fight William to establish the truth.

Dispense with noble visions of knights in shining armour, white steeds, lances and battle-axes. That was showcase stuff. Trial by battle generally entailed the combatants being dressed in ordinary drab civvies, often unarmed, or at best given a wooden club or a sandbag to swing.

The rules were simple. They fought to the death or nightfall, whichever came first. If both men still stood as the stars came out, then the accuser was said to have lost and was labelled a perjurer. The only other option was for either party to give up by crying 'craven', but, as this amounted to losing the battle and accepting the resulting punishment, it was scarcely a popular choice.

Hugh Bolare didn't crave mercy, but nor did he perish during the fight. He saw the stars over Carlisle that night but so too did William the Long. Both men survived the conflict. Perhaps it was no more than 'codpieces at ten paces'.

But, as it was Hugh who had brought the case by falsely accusing William of selling him the ox, the court was bound to brand Hugh the perjurer and he was duly hanged. So was it 'Gilbert the Goose's' ox? Only the ox knew the truth – but he wasn't talking.

There is a curious postscript to this case. Although trial by battle fell largely into disuse by the end of the thirteenth century, the practice was, like many 'laws', never formally wiped from the statute books.

Thus it was that a judge in Warwickshire shifted uneasily in his chair in 1818 when a defendant found not guilty of murdering a girl was confronted, on the pronouncement of the verdict, by the fair maiden's brother noisily accusing him afresh. As a consequence, the defendant entered a legal time warp and cried, 'I am not guilty and this I am ready to defend with my body!'

The judge manfully managed to avert such an anachronistic spectacle and a year later in 1819 Lord Chancellor Eldon moved in the House of Lords that trial by battle be abolished. The bill was agreed to without a word of opposition and indeed witnesses have written that 'the Lords were dumbstruck with astonishment' that such a supposedly obsolete matter should be the subject of debate at all.

So now it is much safer to be a two-ox family, although, strangely enough, lawyers about to face each other in court can still sometimes be heard to talk of 'doing battle'.

THE ACCUSED
HAVE GONE TO GROUND
STELVIO, ITALY, 1519

Five centuries ago it was a far less secure life being part of the animal kingdom than it is now. No television vets to promote the cuddly image of God's creatures. Just a society that saw animals as equally capable of committing crime as humans and a legal system fully equipped to try them and hang them if the need arose.

It may seem like making mountains out of molehills, and that was certainly the case at Stelvio in northern Italy in 1519, when the authorities decided that damage done to crops in the vicinity of the town was an act of pure wanton destruction.

The identity of the culprits was obvious and a warrant was promptly issued to summon a number of moles, which the court desired 'should show cause for their conduct by pleading their exigencies and distress'.

The moles, while quite evidently vandals of the lowest order, must have had a modicum of intelligence because they cunningly failed to turn up at their trial on the appointed day.

The court passed judgment in their absence and the moles were sentenced to exile, although as an act of mercy they were promised safe conduct on their journey 'and an additional respite of 14 days to all those who are with young'.

But, even as the sentence was read, the pesky burrowers were already shovelling like blazes, making their great escape, ready to pop up in some other poor devil's field to create the same havoc all over again. Little varmints!

Nor is this by any means an isolated case. In May 1545 the residents of St Julien in France held a mass trial of vine weevils when their precious wine crop was destroyed. The beetles had their own lawyer, Pierre Falcon, but he failed to bring home their case.

It seems pigs were the real delinquents of the animal kingdom. Records show that 34 were executed for the murder of children, and the porcine culprits were often dressed in human clothing for their court appearances before being publicly hanged or burnt at the stake.

Astonishingly, the notion of animals as criminals survived until the end of the nineteenth century, and the last known such trial was in Switzerland in 1906, when two men and a dog were tried for robbing and killing a man. The men got life but the dog was condemned to death.

One supposes we have moved on. Now we may prosecute the owners of troublesome beasts and order that the worst offending creatures be 'put down', but the idea of animals or birds being 'tried' as such seems ludicrous.

Nonetheless, that doesn't stop the animal kingdom occasionally making legal headlines even in our more enlightened times. Take the case heard at Oxford Crown Court on 9 October 1992. Mark Leach, the accused, had suffered neighbour trouble going right back to 1988, when Susan and Paddy Williams moved in next door – with two parrots.

The incessant squawking drove Leach to distraction and he responded first in kind by using a football rattle to create a rival racket. Still the parrots squawked and relations reached an all-time low in March 1992, when Leach and his wife Dolores decided enough was enough.

They kicked down the garden fence and marched on the aviary. Then, amid a flurry of feathers and spine-chilling screeching, Leach strangled one of the birds. Not content merely with parroticide, he bit Williams on the thigh as he tried to intervene. It was too late, though, for the poor feathered wretch had been dispatched to meet his maker.

In court, Leach admitted the strangling and to damaging property, for which he was fined £600 and ordered to pay £350 costs, but not before his defence, David Osborne, had played a 30-second tape to the court in which the squawking of the inconsiderate but now sadly dead parrot had been registered in his prime at nearly 90 decibels.

This is believed to be the only case of an ex-parrot (not a Norwegian Blue, as far as I'm aware) being called to give evidence in a court of law. Maybe we're not as far removed from the sixteenth-century Italians as we like to think.

AN IMAGINATIVE CONFESSION

NORTH BERWICK, SCOTLAND, 1590

It was Queen Elizabeth I (1533–1603) who first highlighted witchcraft as an official crime in 1563, but it was James VI of Scotland, later James I of England (1566–1625), whose hatred of 'these detestable slaves of the Devil' soared to such heights that scores of innocent women were put to horrific death during his reign.

The witch-hunt at North Berwick in 1590 is one of the most famous of his culls and gave rise to what must be a candidate for the most outlandish confession of all time.

Accused of being a witch, Agnes Sampson was brought before King James himself for interrogation. He had a particular downer on these 'instruments of Satan' at that time because he was convinced that witches were to blame for saddling him with the wedding arrangements from hell.

Twice in November 1589, his bride-to-be, 16-year-old Princess Anne of Denmark, had set sail across the North Sea to join him for the nuptials in Scotland, but twice she was forced back by violent storms. Naturally, James, being a red-blooded 23-year-old, became a tad frustrated. It was obviously the work of witches. So James decided to sail for Denmark himself, hand-picking several ladies-in-waiting to present to his bride. One drowned crossing the River Leith. The 'evil enchanters' had struck yet again before the wedding party was even under way.

His voyage across the North Sea was a rough one (damn

witches!) and when he finally landed at Uppsala and clapped his lustful eyes on the Princess his initial amorous overtures were rejected. No prizes for guessing who was to blame.

Eventually, after 'a few words privily spoken', James and Anne hit it off, were married, and settled in Scotland, but only after his ship had almost foundered on the journey home. If there'd been a wedding video it would certainly have turned out blank. Why wouldn't the old hags leave him be?

By now James had become obsessed with the evil ways of witches, making a deep personal study of the subject and vowing 'to prove that such diveelish artes have been and still are in existence and to exact the trial and severe punishment they merite'.

Poor Agnes Sampson was one of the first to be rounded up. James was determined she would confess to witchcraft. A rope was twisted around her forehead and progressively tightened as an aide-mémoire.

'It was me who called the maelstrom to your ship after your marriage,' she confessed. 'I cast a cat into the sea with parts of a dead body to raise a storm.'

That was mere junior witchcraft as far as James was concerned. The rope was twisted afresh. Agnes needed inspiration: 'One All Hallows' Eve myself and 200 other witches went to sea.' Mere standard fodder: 'We sailed up the Firth from North Berwick to Leith in a magic sieve,' she added with a gleam in her eye. James seemed to warm to this one but still wanted more: 'Then we landed back here at North Berwick and danced in this manner.' Cue manic contortions.

But the royal torturer remained sceptical. Agnes went for the big one: 'We went to North Berwick Church and there met the Devil. He made us kiss his buttocks and swear hostility to the King of Scotland and he declared Your Majesty to be the greatest enemy he had in the world.'

It was good. Too good for James. He wasn't keen on the

last bit: 'You witches are all extreame lyars,' he is reported to have said according to transcripts from the *Newes of Scotland*. Another twist of the rope was applied.

Having thus overegged the pudding Agnes, described by a witness as 'no common or sordid hag, but a grave and douce matron who gave serious and discreet answers', took a more cerebral approach.

She took the King aside and whispered in his ear what she claimed to be the very words that had privily passed between him and his wife on their wedding night. It must have been an inspired guess, for we are told that at last 'the King wondered greatly and swore by the living God that he believed all the devils in hell could not have discovered the same, for the words were most true'.

Agnes's confession had at last passed muster. She had triumphed. As a reward for this the rope around her forehead was blessedly loosened. But, as a reward for now being a proven witch, she was soundly thrashed and burnt at the stake at Haddington in 1591!

Being a suspected witch in the reign of James VI was no joke. He spent much of his time thereafter looking for the signs and wrote a treatise, *The Daemonologie*, on the subject in 1597. His Witchcraft Act of 1603 was responsible for many more deaths and being a witch remained a capital offence until the Witchcraft Act of 1735. It is no longer possible in law to 'be a witch' in the old sense, for that act was repealed in 1961.

But beware all ye who seek to dabble in 'matters occult' for it was replaced in that year by the Fraudulent Mediums Act. Even in these enlightened post-James days both 'susceptibility to' and 'suspicion of' supposedly supernatural powers are alive and well. You have been warned.

A DELAYED DECISION

LONDON, 1613

'An incompetent attorney can delay a trial for years or months. A competent attorney can delay one even longer.'

When the Attorney General of California, Evelle J. Younger, delivered that somewhat cynical line in the *Los Angeles Times* in March 1971 he was merely echoing what those who earn a living from the legal profession have known since time immemorial. There's little to be gained from hurrying.

It follows that legal history is replete with long, drawn-out cases but this one from 1613 was the slow-burner of all time.

It was James I (1566–1625), that 'wisest fool in Christendom', who started it. Such were his absurdly high views of the royal prerogative that he was prepared to go to great lengths to secure for the Crown by legal action what he felt rightly ought to be his. In 1613 the particular object of his desire was the ancient site of Smithfield market. But, ever since he succeeded Elizabeth I to the English throne in 1603, people had been telling him the market wasn't his. There were pretty solid rumours that it had been granted by charter to the citizens of the City of London back in the fifteenth century. James wasn't having that.

The subsequent court action brought by the Crown was intended to establish their ownership once and for all, but hopes of a quickie were soon dispelled. While the Crown

Commissioners brought forth evidence that the site was part of the royal demesne way back in the fourteenth century, the opposition would keep banging on about later charters granted by Henry VI and Henry VII, which ceded the site to 'the Mayor, Commonalty and citizens of the City of London'.

Against such determined arguments James was advised to let it drop, at least for the time being, and the action of *The Crown v. The City of London* was duly stayed by consent in 1614, a year after it had begun. Proceedings were thus suspended.

It was Mr Justice Hoffman who next weighed the evidence when the case was reopened and he pronounced judgment with a certitude that none of his predecessors had been able to muster: 'Indeed the site was part of the royal demesne until early in the fifteenth century,' he said, 'but Smithfield was indubitably included in land later given to the City under charter granted by Henry VI in 1444 and confirmed by Henry VII in 1505.'

It seemed a resounding defeat for the Crown, yet James I didn't turn a hair. He might well have turned in his grave, though, as by then he'd been dead 367 years. For when Justice Hoffman gave his ruling in the High Court the calendar that day read 6 May 1992.

The time-warp case of all time had resurfaced as a result of the City Corporation's approval in April of plans for a £50 million redevelopment programme to bring the historic meat market in line with EC food-hygiene regulations. A far cry from 1613.

A delay of 368 years to resolve a simple land ownership dispute is some going. Lawyers being mindful of inflation, legal fees were sensibly adjusted in an upward direction to prove what they have known for centuries. It pays not to rush things.

JURY v. BENCH
THE OLD BAILEY, LONDON, 1670

It's certainly unusual for a jury to challenge the authority of the learned legal personages on the bench, but that was exactly what happened in the trial of Penn and Mead in London in 1670. The incident changed the course of legal history in favour of a fair trial for the common man.

On Sunday, 14 August 1670, in Gracechurch Street, London, the English Quaker leader William Penn, then a law scholar, teamed up with a former law student, William Mead, for a spot of gentle street preaching. Nothing manic – it's just not the Quaker way. A crowd soon gathered and presently a couple of London's city officers sidled up, as they do, and promptly arrested Penn and Mead in full flow.

The indictment put before the court when their trial began at the Old Bailey on 1 September 1670 was for 'unlawful assembly'. It spoke dramatically of 'a tumultuous gathering in contempt of the King' causing 'great terror of his people and a gross disturbance of the peace'. In an age of religious intolerance, that was Charles II's way of saying, 'Cut out that Quaker stuff right sharp.'

The nine high-ups on the bench, including the Mayor of London, Sam Starling, may have known they were in for a rough ride when Penn and Mead refused to remove their Quaker hats in court. They were duly given a hefty fine.

The trial commenced and the officers who had made the arrests gave evidence of 'talking' but certainly not of 'tumult, violence and terror'.

Penn's defence was that he had done nothing more than preach peaceably and he demanded to know by what exact instrument he was being prosecuted: 'Upon common law,' replied the recorder, Thomas Howel. 'Then show it me,' challenged Penn.

When Howel failed utterly to cite particular statutes, Penn suggested that he could surely not be expected to plead 'to an indictment that has no foundation in law'. Howel, now somewhat hot under the collar, promptly called him 'a saucy fellow'. The jury looked on. Eyebrows were raised.

Not at all impressed by Penn's continued argument on a 'point of law', the recorder ordered him to be put into a squalid lock-up adjacent the courtroom. That left Mead, rather irregularly, holding the fort.

He plugged away in like manner, but still the recorder was unable to quote the relevant legislation. In the end Mead did it for him, explaining in an aside to the jury that an unlawful assembly 'is when three or more assemble together to do an unlawful act'. Therefore no unlawful assembly, he insisted, had taken place.

The jury mused. Further eyebrows were raised.

For his insolence, Mead too was put in the lock-up and Penn, buoyed up by events, loudly addressed the jury from there. Doors were quickly slammed shut to put an end to that shenanigan as the recorder summed up. He directed the jury that it was a cast-iron case and they retired to consider on 3 September 1670.

Ninety minutes later, just eight of them trooped back into court. The other four refused to come and they were forcibly dragged in. At that point the rebels' leader, Edward Bushel, took the unprecedented step for a juror of daring to challenge the bench: 'We don't countenance the way this whole matter is conducted, sir.'

After labelling him 'a troublesome and divisive fellow', Recorder Howel insisted they retire anew to give 'a proper verdict'. When they returned later, Foreman Bushel pronounced Penn 'guilty of *speaking* in Gracechurch Street'. Nothing more. The recorder made it clear that the jury were fudging the issue and that they must say 'guilty' or 'not guilty' without qualification: 'Go and consider it once more,' he thundered. Again the jury returned. This time they found Mead 'not guilty' but again fudged on Penn. The recorder's response was to lock the jury up for the night, then a standard practice, until they gave a valid verdict. Or, in truth, one he liked. Namely 'guilty' full stop.

They emerged tired and hungry at 7a.m. the next day but with their resolve intact. Their verdict on Penn was unchanged.

Again they were sent out. Again they came back and again Edward Bushel returned the same verdict.

The bench lost patience: 'I'll fine you, Edward Bushel,' raged Recorder Howel; 'Cut off his nose!' chipped in the mayor, warming to the fray.

Penn seized his chance to say his bit: 'What hope is there of ever having justice done when juries are threatened and their verdicts rejected?'

Howel was unmoved: 'The jury will go out again,' he warned, 'and deliver another verdict, else they will starve and will be dragged around the city as in Edward Ill's time.'

Out they went for the fourth time and after yet another night locked up without food and water they returned next morning, 5 September 1670, to deliver a historic pronouncement: 'Our verdict is changed, sir,' said Foreman Bushel.

The recorder must have thought they'd cracked, but not a bit of it: 'Both men are not guilty,' said Bushel.

That signalled the end of a bizarre trial, but not of the story, for the jury was fined heavily and put in Newgate Prison. Penn and Mead were fined for contempt of court and sent to join them but they were freed when Penn's father paid the fines.

Edward Bushel, meanwhile, the most defiant juror of all time, appealed to the Chief Justice and ably told the full sorry saga of the bench bullies.

Chief Justice Vaughan found entirely in the jury's favour: 'A jury must be independently and inscrutably responsible for its verdict free from any threat from the court,' he pronounced, before releasing the heroic 12 forthwith.

Bushel and his fellow jurors had stood steadfastly against the worst excesses of kangaroo-court justice and all who have been tried since have something to thank them for. In the hall of London's Central Criminal Court, the world-famous Old Bailey, is a plaque paying tribute to that trusty jury of 1670, ensuring that this strange but seriously pivotal case will never be forgotten.

A TOUCH OF THE BLARNEY
THE TOWER OF LONDON, 1671

It would be difficult to conceive of a more hopeless situation than the one facing Colonel Thomas Blood in 1671. At a time when treason was punishable by a certain and gruesome death he had committed the supremely symbolic and perhaps most overtly treasonable act of all: he'd half-inched the crown jewels.

What's more, he'd been caught red-handed and faced a personal audience with King Charles II, the 'Merry Monarch', who would no doubt cheerfully condemn the wretched Blood to an even more wretched end. To cap it all, poor Thomas had no legal representation. Blood was certainly on the carpet.

No sane betting man would have put money on his walking away unscathed. Yet he was granted a complete pardon, had all his forfeited estates restored and lived a prosperous and influential future life at the heart of the King's court with a personal pension of £500 per annum thrown in. Blood's great escape was an audacious one indeed.

Thomas Blood was born in Ireland around 1618 and, by the time Oliver Cromwell defeated Charles II at Worcester in 1651, sending the monarch into exile in France, he had become fiercely anti-royalist and game for a scrap in support of that cause whenever the opportunity arose. His reward for sundry acts of treachery was a handsome portfolio of Irish landed estates, formerly the property of the King. The rental returns were substantial. When Charles regained the throne by the Restoration in 1660, Blood's ill-gotten gains were promptly taken back from him. He was dispossessed at a stroke, and in turn *became* possessed by the undying desire to wreak vengeance on the monarchy for condemning him to such poverty and loss of face.

He harboured the grudge for fully 11 years and early in 1671 he decided to commit the most scandalous crime of all. He first befriended the rather elderly deputy keeper at the Tower of London, a man named Talbot Edwards, whose job it was to guard the crown jewels. Early in the morning of 9 May, Blood used his acquaintance with the gullible Edwards to gain access to the strongroom. While his accompanying gang made off with the orb, sceptre and other regalia, Blood took the supreme prize, the crown itself.

But the escape wasn't well planned. With the crown stuffed under his cloak, Blood got no further than a few hundred yards before his getaway horse slipped and fell. He was quickly arrested and taken back to the tower, this time as a prisoner rather than a souvenir hunter.

Never had a man's future looked grimmer. But Blood was a cheeky so-and-so, and his cockiness in the face of certain personal disaster amazingly paid handsome dividends.

His capture was the talk of all London. Everybody looked forward to a sensational trial and celebrity execution. But Blood played it cute. As soon as he was arrested he refused to say anything to any of his interrogators, except that he would speak only to the King himself.

Charles was amused and intrigued by such an unconventional request and Blood was duly ushered before the royal presence. He admitted all in a charming and smarmy manner. He then warned His Majesty in the most helpful tone of the consequences of an execution: 'Consider, Your Majesty, that my accomplices are still at large,' he said, 'and may well wreak the ultimate vengeance upon your person.'

Then he played his master stroke, explaining to Charles that he had once been at the very point of assassinating him but had held back at the last moment: 'Although you were at my mercy, bathing unprotected in the Thames at Battersea, the sight of Your Majesty filled me with such awe I was unable to do you any harm.'

More syrupy pronouncements from this consummate licker followed in quick succession and Charles, suitably impressed by such a bold approach and with his ego massively boosted, promptly gave Blood a full pardon. His estates and income were swiftly restored and the only court Thomas Blood appeared in was that of the King, where he swanked for all he was worth and became the talk of all London yet again.

As a demonstration of the art of self-defence, with not a lawyer in sight, Blood's performance was one of the most masterly in history. The Irishman who stole the crown jewels had employed nothing more than a touch of the blarney to escape from the tightest corner in legal history.

WELL, I'LL BE HANGED!
TYBURN GALLOWS, LONDON, 1705

On a small traffic island near the junction of London's Edgware Road and Oxford Street is an unobtrusive plaque bearing the words HERE STOOD TYBURN TREE, REMOVED 1759. What tales that site could tell, for it was there that a permanent gallows, a large triangular structure with three overhead beams known as the Triple Tree, was used to hang as many as 24 men at a time in front of baying holiday crowds.

Yet, of all its tales, one is more remarkable than most. This is the case of John Smith, whose unexceptional name belies the quite exceptional story of survival that was to make him one of the leading criminal celebrities of his age.

A native of Malton, near York, Smith settled in London early in the eighteenth century after spending some years at sea. Once on dry land, he enlisted in the Second Regiment of Foot Guards but soon embarked on a life of habitual crime, by no means unusual for a soldier at that time.

Soon enough, he was in big trouble with the law. On 3 December 1705 he was apprehended on suspicion of breaking and entering and two days later was arraigned at the Old Bailey on four separate indictments. Each involved theft; valuable quantities of shoes, cloth, China silk and gloves were the booty, and each was a capital offence.

Although Smith, then in his forties, managed to talk his way out of blame for two of the alleged offences, he was found guilty of the two others. He had, after all, been caught red-handed on the premises with 148 pairs of gloves ready to go. It was a clumsy burglary attempt and his explanation that he was all fingers and thumbs was a futile one.

He was sentenced to death and incarcerated in the Condemned Hold of Newgate Prison, where he vainly hoped for a reprieve, which didn't come. At least not yet.

On 12 December he was carted to Tyburn, strung up and turned off the wagon to swing. The hangman pulled his legs for good measure, a merciful act intended to prevent undue suffering, for all hangings prior to the nineteenth century were of the 'short-drop' variety involving a fall of just 3 or 4ft (about 1m) and many victims survived for some considerable time before life finally left them.

That proved to be Smith's salvation, for even the final tug didn't finish him off quickly, although witnesses who say he swung for fully 15 minutes swore that he looked as dead as can be.

As last-minute reprieves go, the one that was then inexplicably and dramatically delivered by a messenger on horseback looked to be a classic case of 'too late was the cry', but Smith was swiftly cut down all the same and conveyed, still apparently lifeless, to a nearby public house.

It was there that John Smith secured his fame. One of the first to be impressed was the diarist Narcissus Luttrell, who wrote: 'He was immediately lett blood and put into a warm bed, which, with other applications, brought him to himself again with much adoe.'

Smith was neither the first nor last man to survive the noose, but what really made his case celebratory was the mileage he subsequently got from his miraculous escape.

When he was taken back to Newgate Prison he quickly became the centre of attention among his fellow prisoners; members of the public queued up and paid to view him as a star exhibit; he related a sensational published account of the hanging itself in which he described 'my spirits in a strange commotion, violently pressing up to my head, then a great blaze of glaring light which seemed to come out of my eyes with a flash before I lost all sense of pain'.

It was all good stuff. Nowadays he'd have employed a PR guru to create the image for him, but John Smith was a natural long before the age of spin, and the hype worked a treat.

His reprieve was followed by an unconditional pardon and he was released from prison on 20 February 1706.

And there his story might end, but, having survived the ultimate penalty, John Smith seemed intent on chancing his arm yet again. Although he kept on the straight and narrow for almost ten years, during which time he kept a pub at Southwark, he was back to his old tricks by January 1715, when he was picked up near Fenchurch Street after breaking into a warehouse. Again it was a capital offence and a date at the Old Bailey beckoned.

But Smith's charmed life continued. He spent 18 months in Newgate but was at length found not guilty on a technicality. And so it went on: further crimes followed in 1720 and 1721, but on the first occasion he was acquitted and for the second offence he again went back to Newgate.

Only in 1727, when he once more transgressed, did the English legal system finally rid itself of the man they called 'half-hanged Smith'. Twenty-two years after his famous Tyburn appearance he was transported, in his sixty-sixth year, to the American colonies.

Had the hangman done his job properly on 12 December 1705, plain old John Smith would be a mere statistic instead of a celebrity criminal akin to a 'soap star' of eighteenth-century society.

Avid strangeologists may be disappointed to know that the late nineteenth-century executioner William Marwood spoilt all the fun when, in 1874, he introduced the merciful 'long-drop' method of hanging, by which the victim had to fall between 6 and 10ft (2–3m) based on a calculation involving their state of health, build and weight.

That sure-fire scientific method seemed certain to signal the end of the grand old age of execution cock-ups. But despair not, for where there's technology the gremlins will surely follow. Turn to 'Three-Times-Lucky Lee' for the ropiest hanging of all time.

MORRISON HEARS IT ALL
EDINBURGH, SCOTLAND, 1721

Catherine Shaw had not been on the best of terms with her father William for some time. Like many before her and since, she found to her annoyance that her choice of young man didn't meet with Dad's approval.

William felt strongly that she had 'encouraged the addresses of a man' whom he intensely disliked as 'a profligate and debauchee'. Words passed between father and daughter on many occasions in the tenement flat they shared in Edinburgh, and on one particular night in the winter of 1721 voices were raised to such a pitch that their neighbour, Mr Morrison, could not help but overhear.

Several times he heard the girl cry the chilling words, 'Cruel father, thou art the cause of my death!' followed finally by awful groaning, then the unmistakable sound of William Shaw leaving the house.

Morrison alerted neighbours as the Shaw residence fell ominously silent, but they could not gain entry. A constable was called to break in and poor Catherine Shaw was found, barely alive, weltering in blood and with a knife by her side: 'Has your father killed you?' they asked. She was unable to speak but seemed to those present to have nodded her head before expiring moments later.

When William Shaw returned he trembled violently as he saw his daughter's dead body. He turned pale. The small gathering started to put two and two together, and four began to look a pretty conclusive answer when the constable noticed traces of blood on Shaw's shirt and hands.

He was quickly put before a magistrate and admitted they had had serious quarrels of late over 'the man business'. But on the night in question, he insisted, he had been in another room and had gone out without harming his daughter in any way. He had himself heard the cries, but dismissed them as mere histrionics. The blood was readily explained: 'Some days since, I was bled by a barber and the bandages came untied that night resulting in stains on my shirt and hands.'

The prosecution majored on the evidence of Morrison. He was absolutely sure of the words he had heard: 'Cruel father, thou art the cause of my death!' Catherine's implicit nodding of her head in her last moments was surely an added proof.

Against such evidence William Shaw was convicted, sentenced and executed at Leith Walk in November 1721 with the full approval of public opinion, although Shaw himself maintained his innocence even on the scaffold.

Only in the New Year did it emerge that Catherine Shaw was something of a drama queen. The new tenant of Shaw's flat found a sheet of paper, which had slipped down an opening near the chimney.

Evidently placed originally on the mantelpiece, it was written in Catherine's hand and addressed to her father. She reproached him in the letter for his barbarity and said she realised she would never marry the man she loved but was determined not to accept a man of her father's choice. She had decided to end her burdensome existence. The letter finished with a flourish: 'My death I lay to your charge. When you read this, consider yourself as the inhuman wretch that plunged the knife into the bosom of the unhappy Catherine Shaw!'

With that parting shot she had taken her own life with full histrionic sound effects. William Shaw may well have been an inhuman wretch but he was undoubtedly an innocent man.

The authorities made a noble attempt at damage limitation, removing his emaciated body from the gibbet where it still hung and giving the wronged man a decent burial. Contemporary reports say that 'a pair of colours was waved over his grave', but no amount of respect could redress the miscarriage of justice.

Had either the key witness, Mr Morrison, or the court been familiar with the device later used to such good effect by Agatha Christie in a number of her novels, the evidence might have been more closely scrutinised.

A disembodied voice heard from a closed room is not always what it seems. Sometimes even two voices don't prove a conversation with Christie around. One person posing as two, or even the cunning use of a tape recording in an empty room, has been employed to baffling effect by the Queen of Crime.

But Morrison wasn't Hercule Poirot. He hadn't heard the voice of William Shaw but Catherine's words implied he was in the room with her.

If this unusual case proves anything, it is surely that murders, like children, should be seen and not merely heard.

MAGGIE'S REPRIEVE
EDINBURGH, SCOTLAND, 1724

'You are to be taken from this place to a place of execution and there you will be hanged by the neck until you are dead. May the Lord have mercy on your soul.'

Those most chilling words, not heard in Britain since the passing of the Murder (Abolition of Death Penalty) Act 1965, were once commonplace in British courts.

Margaret Dickson heard them in an Edinburgh courtroom on 3 August 1724. So did the jury and all others present at the High Court of Justiciary that day. The finality of that pronouncement could not be denied, yet three centuries later those very words still echo hauntingly, still seem to linger on the long-dead judge's lips, for the case of Margaret Dickson is an odd one indeed.

It was the discovery of a newborn baby's body in the River Tweed at Maxwellheugh, near Kelso, on 9 December 1723, that started it. It was Margaret Dickson's child. Having been deserted by her husband, she had left her two other children behind in Musselburgh, near Edinburgh, and headed south to visit an aunt in Newcastle. She had an extended break in her journey at the small village of Maxwellheugh and there took work with the Bell family. It was one of the Bells' sons who made the gruesome discovery.

Questioning soon revealed that it was Margaret's baby and that she had managed to keep the pregnancy secret from all but the father. Her story was that he was William Bell, another son, who had forced himself on her one night in a drunken stupor. The baby, she said, had been stillborn. She had kept it in her bed for eight days, frantic with worry, before throwing it in the river out of sheer distraction.

It was plausible, but Dickson's secretive manner told against her. Despite her decent and God-fearing Protestant background, she was charged with murder, found guilty, heard the death sentence read, and was hanged in Edinburgh on 2 September 1724.

A baying crowd of thousands witnessed the drop at the Gallows Stone in the Grassmarket. The hangman tugged at her legs for good measure as she swung, and after half an hour she was cut down and placed in a coffin to be taken back to Musselburgh by her friends on a cart.

Scarcely had they left the Edinburgh outskirts before they were attacked by a gang of body snatchers – surgeons' apprentices seeking booty for dissection. They fought the gang off, but not before the coffin had been disturbed and the lid loosened.

They pressed on as far as the village of Peppermill and, still somewhat shaken, stopped there for refreshment. Only then did two passing joiners hear a noise from the coffin, which was duly opened with haste. First, Margaret Dickson's limbs twitched. Then Peter Purdie, one of her friends, opened a vein and a strangled cry of 'Oh dear!' came from Margaret's deathly pale lips. Oh dear indeed.

On 6 September 1724, the Sunday after being hanged, and looking remarkably well considering, she attended church in Musselburgh amid much sensation. She became a great local celebrity and some months later remarried her former husband. Many a man has dreamed of putting new life into his marriage but Margaret's man surely hit the jackpot.

No attempt was made to arrest her again, as Scottish law deemed the sentence to have been fully carried through. Some said it was an act of God, atoning for a crime she didn't commit. In truth it was a slovenly hangman, a loose coffin lid, a couple of nosey joiners and the remarkable resilience of the human body that gave her the incredible second chance.

No one except Margaret Dickson ever knew the real truth about the body in the river, but everyone said she was the luckiest woman alive. Or dead, as the case may be.

AND THE WINNER IS ...
CARLISLE, 1746

When Prince Charles Edward Stuart (1720–88), 'Bonnie Prince Charlie', landed from France on the island of Eriskay in the Outer Hebrides on 23 June 1745, he set in motion a chain of events that has become one of the most famous in British history.

His rebellious march south with intent to claim the English throne was to end in defeat for himself, but also in escape. But for many of his rebel forces fate was less kind, being decided by one of the strangest judicial practices in legal history. Anyone fancy their chances at trial by lottery?

Thomas Coppock was one of those who met their gruesome end in that bizarre fashion. He joined the band of rebel forces at Manchester as the 'Young Pretender' marched south towards London, but the closer to the capital they got the more their numbers dwindled. Ever more depleted and in low spirits, they got no further than the Midlands, being repelled at Derby on 6 December 1745. Some say they were merely repelled 'by' Derby and decided the south just wasn't for them. That's one for debate, but at any rate they retreated north, hotly pursued by the Duke of Cumberland, and ultimate defeat was delivered on 16 April 1746 at Culloden.

Now for the trials. But with almost 400 rebels imprisoned at Carlisle Castle on charges of treason, each requiring a separate hearing, it was more than the courts could cope with. There was nothing for it but trial by lottery!

The procedure was simple but nerve-jangling, and the prize horrific. Prisoners willing to admit their guilt were split into groups of 20 and asked to draw numbers from a hat. The dubious bounty for the one 'winning' ticket was a trial, with its inevitable result. The other 19 men were 'rewarded' by transportation for life, not always in itself a hugely attractive prospect, it is true, but better than sure-fire death.

With a 19-to-one chance of saving their skin, submitting themselves to the lottery was a chance many men took. The Reverend Thomas Coppock, the Oxford-educated chaplain of the rebel forces, was one such, but as he dipped his hand into the hat in September 1746 he was to find that he truly was God's chosen one.

Charged with high treason after conducting a service for the 'Bonnie Prince' in Derby, and already having admitted his guilt, he bore slim hopes of coming out of the trial intact. They were even slimmer when his counsel, a Mr Clayton, failed to turn up to face the five members of the Bar leading the prosecution on behalf of the English Crown. A Scots advocate, David Graham, stepped into the breach to defend him, but neither he nor his client did much to help their cause, as a contemporary account of the trial relates:

Coppock's counsel said very little in regard to his defence, for the prisoner's behaviour before the court was rude and insolent and impudent beyond imagination.

The jury took less than a minute to find Coppock guilty of high treason, which ensured he would meet his end in a fashion even more dreadful than hanging. The judge pronounced sentence: 'You are to be hanged by the neck, but not till you are dead, for you are to be cut down alive, your privy parts cut off and your bowels taken out and burned before your face, your head severed and your body divided into four parts; and those to be at the King's disposal. And the Lord have mercy on your soul.'

Coppock was duly collected on 18 October 1746. He was dragged on a black hurdle from Carlisle Castle to the gallows on Harrowby Hill overlooking the town. Although he kept his composure and delivered a highly treasonable seven-minute sermon as his parting shot, it was there, so to speak, that he finally went to pieces.

Being hung, drawn and quartered fell into blessed disuse after 1746, as did the drawing of lots, but that was scant consolation for the unfortunate Thomas Coppock, winner of the worst lottery prize of all time.

A FISH OUT OF WATER
CARLISLE ASSIZES, 1776

Many critics of the legal system have bemoaned the tendency
of judges and barristers to bamboozle the layman by use of
language. Erudite, jargonistic, Latinised, fanciful or plain
euphemistic, it's an endless conundrum. Just consider the
divorce case:

'And when did you and your wife last have relations?'

'That would have been last Christmas when her mother
came to stay, Your Honour.'

It's an old one but it makes the point. How can the ordinary
person even begin to understand the language of the law?

That's why it comes as such a comfort to know that even
those within the profession are occasionally hoisted by their
own petard. Or, in the interests of plain speaking, should I
say caught out at their own game?

One such unusual case was related in his memoirs by
Lord Eldon, Lord Chancellor for 26 years at the start of the
nineteenth century, and it shows how the use of language,
even at the most basic level, can paralyse the opposition
into submission against their will.

It was at the Carlisle Assizes in 1776 when Eldon, then
just a young practitioner on the Northern Circuit working
as plain John Scott, was called upon to defend a man
accused of salmon poaching. Scott had a yen for such
cases, for although he was to rise to become one of the most
celebrated English lawyers of his era, he had been born of

humble parentage in Newcastle and had a down-to-earth approach that served him well.

Prosecuting the poacher was a barrister named Bearcroft, rather a star in London, who agreed to make his first ever visit to Cumberland only on agreeing the then enormous fee of 300 guineas. Despite his misgivings about the ways of the far north, Bearcroft confidently expected to bring the case home against the country bumpkins. As it was, he got a rude awakening.

John Scott displayed a canny grasp of the power of language by playing on Bearcroft's lack of a common touch – while conducting his defence he spoke in the broad Cumberland dialect of the Carlisle region and liberally scattered his speeches with vernacular phrases, which the jury fully understood but which the increasingly bewildered Bearcroft could make neither head nor tail of.

The crucial moment came when Scott began to question a witness about salmon caught out of season. Scott knew, as did the witness, that such salmon have white flesh instead of red. He also knew that poachers were in the habit of disguising such illegally caught fish, reddening the flesh by smoking it up a chimney to make what were known locally as 'old soldiers', named after the colour of a soldier's red coat.

Being unaware of country matters, Bearcroft strained to follow the dialogue and when Scott asked the witness, 'Did the salmon make good "ould soldiers"?' the surreal image of an army of fish engaging in battle in their twilight years was more than Bearcroft could stand.

He promptly made the mistake of asking Scott to translate, and Scott's clever but surely entirely just retort won the day in this North-versus-South battle of wits: 'Surely a London counsel marked 300 guineas on his brief can understand a simple thing like that. Furthermore, it is not for me, with a fee of only five guineas to my name, to help a London counsel whose value is evidently 60 times as great as my own.'

Thus put in his place, Bearcroft floundered like a fish out of water as the jury warmed to Scott's plain-talking submissions.

The salmon poacher was quickly acquitted and Bearcroft left Carlisle sorely stung by the experience of his northern excursion, swearing, 'No fee shall ever tempt me to come among such a set of barbarians again.'

A famous triumph for Scott. A salutary lesson for Bearcroft. But above all a victory for the plain-speaking society.

I would add only one footnote. One must always be careful of assuming from a response that someone has misunderstood the question. For misconstrual on the grounds of ambiguity can, as a rereading of my opening quotation might suggest, sometimes be a two-way affair.

Who's to say, after all, that it wasn't 'last Christmas', poor chap?

A UNIQUE ASSASSINATION

THE HOUSE OF COMMONS, LONDON, 1812

Every murder is unique. Each victim, after all, is different. But the classification of murders into distinctive types lends a certain commonplace air even to some of the foulest acts. A classic example of the adage, 'familiarity breeds contempt'. But it was not John Bellingham's aim in life to be a commonplace murderer and those present at his trial at the Old Bailey in May 1812 saw the 42-year-old from St Neot's, Huntingdonshire, convicted of a crime that was, and remains to this day, unique in British history. John Bellingham assassinated the Prime Minister.

The esteemed victim, Spencer Perceval, was a Londoner who chose the law as a profession and was called to the bar in 1786. After acting for the government in a number of high-profile cases he was earmarked by Prime Minister William Pitt for higher things and he rose via the office of Attorney General and Chancellor of the Exchequer to become Prime Minister in 1809. Perceval was a Tory but no hint of scandal or sleaze ever tainted his name and he was a family man of high honour – 10 Downing Street echoed to the sound of 11 children during his stay in office. 'Little P', as he became known, was seemingly a thoroughly nice chap; sure, he had vitriolic opponents, but in truth not a serious enemy in the world.

Except John Bellingham. Tall and bony with a long, thin face, Bellingham was a clerk who had worked for years in a

London counting house before branching out to take jobs in Russia and then Hull, where he hoped to make money importing timber. Alas, his Russian contacts let him down and Bellingham suffered huge financial losses, which led him to a spell in prison. It was from his cell that he first began the campaign of blame that was to lead to his immortality as an assassin, and his criticism of the Russian authorities after his release was such that he was soon put behind bars in that country too.

From there he sent letter after letter of complaint to the British ambassador demanding intervention for his release, but all to no avail. Bellingham's rage rose to fever pitch and he determined that, on his release, someone would pay.

On his return to England his campaign to clear his name and seek what he genuinely believed to be his right to compensation continued relentlessly. Again, he got nowhere and when a Whitehall civil servant one day told him to 'go to the Devil, and take whatever action you like!' that was enough to tip Bellingham over the edge.

Straightaway he stalked to a gunsmith's shop in the Strand, spent four guineas on two pistols and ammunition and passed the rest of the day in target practice on Primrose Hill.

For several days afterwards he lurked around the entrance and lobby to the House of Commons staking out the lie of the land, and on Monday, 11 May 1812, he struck the blow that none before or since has dared to emulate.

It was a fine day and Spencer Perceval, in times far less security-conscious than our own, walked to the Commons from 10 Downing Street rather than take a carriage. It was 5.15 in the afternoon when he entered the lobby and from behind a pillar John Bellingham emerged.

In full view of a crowd of constituents and sightseers, the crazed assassin raised a pistol and fired at close range into Perceval's chest. As the Prime Minister lurched forward gasping, 'I am murdered,' Bellingham was seized without a struggle and as Perceval was pronounced dead at the scene Bellingham addressed police: 'I am the unfortunate man who has shot Mr Perceval. My name is John Bellingham. I know what I have done. It was a private injury, a denial of justice on the part of the government.'

Amid a climate of sensation and outrage, Bellingham was taken to Newgate Prison and stood trial at the Old Bailey later that week, at seven o'clock on Friday, 15 May. He pleaded guilty and he also begged for clemency but, not for the first time, Bellingham's protestations were ignored by authority.

Despite his defence playing the 'insanity' card it took the jury just 15 minutes to find him guilty and the only man ever to assassinate a British prime minister was hanged on the gallows outside Newgate Prison on Monday, 18 May, within a week of his infamous deed.

It was a strange affair indeed but some would say it is even stranger that Spencer Perceval remains a unique victim, bearing in mind the vitriolic state of political affairs in recent years. Oddly, there was a moment in January 1983 when British visitors to Canada might have been forgiven for choking on their breakfast cereal as newspaper headlines there read, MINISTERIAL HORROR: MURDER OF MRS THATCHER.

This undeniably eye-catching line turned out to refer to Jo Ann Thatcher, the former wife of Saskatchewan's Minister for Energy and Mines, Colin Thatcher. In another sensational affair it was the minister himself who opted to blow his former wife's brains out in an act of revenge after she had divorced him and won the largest settlement ever awarded by a Canadian court.

What a blessed relief it wasn't the Mrs Thatcher dispatched to keep her fellow Tory, Spencer Perceval, company.

Or do I hear a dissenting voice? Shame on you!

ELEVEN JUST MEN
AND WILSON

CLERKENWELL GREEN, LONDON, 1838

'Juries are like Almighty God ... totally unpredictable,' wrote the barrister and author John Mortimer in his fictional *The Trials of Rumpole* (1979). Had he been writing in 1838, he might well have called the book *The Trials of Adams*.

When Serjeant Adams, chairman of the bench for the Middlesex Sessions, addressed his fellow magistrates at Clerkenwell Green on Tuesday, 2 January 1838, he assured those suffering New Year blues that 'the calendar is unusually light today'.

But his hopes of an easy session were quickly dashed by the presence on the jury of one Mr H. Wilson, whose own eccentric brand of New Year 'resolution' was about to test Adams's patience to hitherto unknown limits.

No sooner had the jury been sworn to try the defendant, Benjamin Dickinson, than Wilson took centre stage: 'I should like to know, Mr Chairman, how I am to be indemnified for my loss of time and the trouble and inconvenience I am put to by coming here.' Adams disdainfully brushed this untimely intervention aside, ordering the deputy clerk, 'Go on with the case.'

'Ay, ay, it's all very well to say "go on" but I won't go on until I know who is to pay me,' whined Wilson in response. Adams replied in patient but firm tone, assuring Wilson that jury service was 'an exceedingly important and essential public duty and one of the most beautiful parts of our admirable constitution for which no remuneration is due', before again ordering the case to proceed.

But yet again the mischievous juryman made the same point and only after several more Wilsonian interruptions of the 'ay, ay' variety did the case proceed.

The evidence against Dickinson for assaulting an officer of the County Court was overwhelming, and Chairman Adams, having finally put Wilson in his proper place, summed up quickly. The jury convened for what should have been an equally rapid decision, but Wilson was game for more.

To the utter exasperation of the jury and all present (except perhaps the accused), he refused to give a verdict without pay. It was time for Chairman Adams to get tough by reminding Wilson that he had sworn under oath to give a verdict: 'And I will place the jury in a locked room without fire or candle until that verdict is delivered,'

At this Wilson remained smilingly uncowed: 'Ay, ay, I have sworn to give a verdict but I did not *say when* or at *what* time. I will do so when I am well and truly ready. Show me the statute that says there is a limit of time or place.'

After more verbal tennis, in which Wilson's argument became ever more semantic, Serjeant Adams ordered an officer to 'remove the jury and lock them in a room until they come to a determination'.

Now it was the rest of the jury who loudly made clear to Adams their disapproval of his orders before turning their attention to Wilson. They reasoned, they pleaded, they cajoled, but all to no avail: 'Oh, let us subscribe and pay him what he wants,' they finally cried in unison, but Chairman Adams would have none of it and again ordered the jury's retention under lock and key.

'I shall not leave this box,' piped Wilson, delivering yet more of the same and a good deal of 'ay, aying' along the way.

'His stubbornness,' wrote *The Times*, 'caused the greatest

confusion and utmost anxiety as he sat tight in a manner which induced a supposition that he would not quit the jury-box.'

Then, just as more court heavies moved in to remove him bodily, Wilson calmly rose amid much nodding and winking to his fellow jurors and jauntily acquiesced to the lock-in. It lasted only 15 minutes and the jury duly delivered a verdict of guilty.

What happened behind the locked door doesn't take much guessing, for Wilson, 'an honest tradesman', emerged much relaxed and smiling contentedly. Evidently, he had got his way.

So what was the price of justice? For Adams a restless night after his brush with the most irritating juror of all time.

And doubtless for Wilson a few tankards of decent ale, a goblet or so of wine and a rather splendid dinner.

A NEW LINE OF ENQUIRY
AYLESBURY ASSIZES, 1845

When John Tawell decided to start the New Year with rather more resolution than was good for him, it led to a chain of events that created legal history, as an overflowing courtroom at Aylesbury Assizes in March 1845 later listened earnestly to the unprecedented and at that time amazing story of Tawell's capture.

It was 1 January 1845 when the 60-year-old Englishman murdered his secret mistress, Sarah Hart, at her cottage in Salt Hill, near Slough, Buckinghamshire. A bottle of porter liberally laced with prussic acid was the last drink Sarah ever shared with her somewhat mature lover.

Tawell's entirely selfish motive was partly that he was afraid that his wife, with whom he lived an apparently respectable life in Berkhamsted, Hertfordshire, would discover his double life. But perhaps even more than that was the need to keep the knowledge of his sordid set-up from fellow Friends of the rather purist Quaker movement, of which he passed himself off as a member.

Tawell was a devious man and had a good escape and alibi planned. He had earlier deposited an overcoat in the cloakroom of the Jerusalem Coffee House in London. After the poisoning he planned to catch the train from Slough to Paddington, from where his movements would be entirely unobserved by the law. From there he would go to the coffee house, collect his coat and claim, if questions were ever asked, that he had been in London for the hours conveniently spanning the murder. No one would ever know. The burgeoning railways were certainly the criminal's friend.

Yet circumstances entirely beyond his control led him to stand trial three months later. That an elderly gentleman in Quaker garb had been spotted leaving the murdered woman's house by a neighbour ought not to have mattered bearing in mind his London alibi, nor that a Quaker had purchased a first-class ticket at Slough station and been seen boarding an early-evening train there, for as word got around that the Quaker might be worth watching Tawell was well on the way to Paddington. Of course it must be another Quaker, for he had been in London all the time.

But, scrupulous planner that he was, John Tawell was not up to press with the newest technology. Fully 37 years before Alexander Graham Bell invented the telephone in 1876, many a criminal's downfall, William Fothergill Cooke and Professor Charles Wheatstone had managed to interest the Great Western Railway in their latest hi-tech electric-telegraph communication system. GWR gave it a try on the Paddington-West Drayton line in 1839 and extended it to Slough in 1843. Tawell, rather a dinosaur in such matters, hadn't figured on its possible uses, yet it proved to be the unlikely source of his downfall.

Even as he settled into his seat on his journey to safety, the telegraph clerk at Slough was wiring Paddington. The system worked perfectly, although the inability of the equipment to transmit the letters Q and U meant the clerk had to alert police to look out for 'a gentleman in the garb of a KWAKER'. Three times he sent the message before the police twigged it – maybe they were looking for someone dressed as a duck. But even primitive telegraph messages travelled faster than the trains and, as Tawell stepped confidently on to Paddington station, a plain-clothes police officer had no difficulty spotting his man.

He was trailed to the Jerusalem Coffee House, observed for the rest of the day and finally arrested next morning. His story and indignant denials got him nowhere, for thanks to the wires it was incontrovertible that the Slough Quaker and the London Quaker were one and the same.

After he was found guilty and condemned to be hanged he admitted all and before the fatal day many more details of Tawell's double life emerged. Banknote forgery, transportation to Australia and other suspicious deaths all came to light. Tawell was well and truly discredited and a contemporary record tartly reported that 'a respectable garb, sedate demeanour and outward benevolence have seldom concealed a more wicked and unprincipled heart'.

As the first man to be convicted with the aid of the electric telegraph, Tawell, by his unlikely demise, served to deliver a timely warning to all future criminals. If you want to get away with it don't be a technophobe and don't dress as a Quaker.

NO, NO, NO, NO, NO ... YES
GLAMORGAN QUARTER SESSIONS, 1853

Only the harshest critic would deny that the task of a jury
in deciding a verdict can be a very difficult one indeed. But,
once the foreman of the jury rises to deliver that verdict,
then that part of the procedure is surely simplicity itself.
Nay, even foolproof. He must pronounce 'guilty' or 'not
guilty'. Nothing could possibly go wrong.

Strange, then, that the leading case of *The Crown v.*
William Vodden, heard at Glamorgan Quarter Sessions in
1853, should ever have entered the legal textbooks, let alone
be cited on a number of occasions since, even as recently
as 1999.

But cited it is, for jury foremen, it seems, sometimes get a
little befuddled. The (possibly apocryphal!) case of the Irish
foreman who confidently announced, 'My Lord, we find
the man who stole the mare not guilty' is not as ludicrous
as it may seem, nor is the celebrated procrastination of
Tony Hancock in a classic episode of television's *Hancock's*
Half Hour.

In the Glamorgan case, Vodden was on trial for larceny,
that quaint old term for theft that makes that act sound
almost artistic. At the end of proceedings the jury foreman,
Owen Hughes, rose to deliver the clear verdict of not guilty.
The chairman duly discharged the prisoner but as he did
so there was an audible murmur from the remainder of
the jury. They had, they quickly made clear, all agreed on a

verdict of guilty. As a result of this confusion the defendant was brought back into the dock and the chairman of the bench subjected the jury to a round of 'Is that your final answer?' The first 11 said the intended verdict was definitely guilty and when it came to Owen Hughes he too, perhaps too embarrassed to admit his inexplicable slip of the tongue, said he had definitely said 'Guilty'.

As a consequence, the erstwhile and much relieved defendant was cast into a rather darker humour as the verdict was reversed and he was sentenced to two months' hard labour.

That being a somewhat unpleasant prospect, he decided to appeal for a counter-reversal and the case went to the Court for Crown Cases Reserved. There Chief Baron Pollock established an important precedent: 'What happened was a daily occurrence in the ordinary transactions of life,' he said, 'namely that a mistake was made but then corrected within a reasonable time, and on the very spot on which it was made.' He ruled that the hard labour must stand.

The message to jurors was clear. If you botch it up, admit it pronto. Strange as it is that the wrong wording from a choice of only two verdicts should ever emerge from the mouth of a jury foreman at the crucial moment, the precedent established by the Vodden case has been put to the test throughout legal history. In 1985, in *The Crown v. Andrews*, the jury foreman clearly announced a verdict of not guilty on the charge that the defendant had subjected a child to cruelty. But ten minutes later, during the sentencing of a co-defendant, he sheepishly passed a note to the judge stating: 'We thought we found Andrews guilty; what happens now?' It may sound like an entertaining alternative to *A Question of Sport*, but it was all in deadly earnest and again, much to Andrews's disgust, an about-turn was ordered and a verdict of guilty was recorded. The Court of Appeal later once more upheld the Vodden principle and the guilty verdict held.

Only where there has been too lengthy a time lapse in such

cases or a change of mind has been deemed to be purely on a whim has the Court of Appeal ordered 'erroneous' first verdicts to stand.

If only juries were perfect such debates would be non-existent, and *The Law's Strangest Cases* would be a very slim volume, which would never do. So, thank goodness that folly among jurors is an established part of legal history.

Take the farcical goings-on at Snaresbrook Crown Court in 1993. After listening for three days to the case against a man accused of robbery, the jury deliberated their verdict for three hours before losing the plot completely and sending a note to the judge, which asked, 'Is it a question of whether we have to decide if he is guilty or not guilty?'

Nor is the mayhem confined to home shores. In 1960 an Appeal Court in New Jersey, USA, ordered a retrial in an accident case because of 'basic confusion' in the original courtroom. The final straw came, so it seems, when the judge asked the jury foreman, 'Have you agreed on your verdict, Mr Foreman?' The reply – 'My name isn't Foreman: my name is Admerman' – was more than the judge could bear.

And the great thing about these oddities is that, just when you think they can't get any worse, they do.

Back in the realms of the guilty-or-not-guilty conundrum, we again find ourselves in Wales. At Cardiff Crown Court in April 1999 Judge Michael Gibbon sentenced Alan Rashid, charged with making a threat to kill, to two years' imprisonment, after he thought he heard the jury foreman say 'Guilty'. Only when a confused juror asked an usher to explain the sentence did it emerge that 'Not guilty' was the intended verdict. Tapes of the proceedings were played and Rashid was duly freed. Surprise, surprise: no appeal from the accused this time!

The story that appeared in all the newspapers was that an untimely cough had drowned out the vital 'not' when the verdict had been delivered, although Judge Gibbon, perhaps keen not to make a monkey of himself, said that had not been the case. The foreman had, quite simply, he asserted, made a mistake in his delivery. Was there a cough? There was certainly a hiccup.

Lord Devlin (1905–92) once learnedly commented, 'What makes juries worthwhile is that they see things differently from judges. Trial by jury is the lamp that shows that freedom lives.' He might well have added, 'Once in a while there is a loose connection in that lamp or the bulb goes out. Then, regrettably, we are all left in the dark.'

THE ELEVENTH WITNESS
MILWAUKEE, UNITED STATES, 1855

Some of the law's oddest cases relate to mistaken identity
and there is no shadow of a doubt that innocent men have
been sentenced, sometimes even to death, on the misguided
assertion of a witness that 'this is definitely the one'.

Studies of the phenomenon have been made and
controlled experiments have shown that the brain's capacity
to absorb, store and later retrieve an image to match to a
perceived likeness is by no means infallible. Sometimes,
too, the rare existence of a genuine double, the near-perfect
doppelgänger, has led to unavoidable errors of identification
and it is for such reasons that the police are apt to seek
safety in numbers if enough witnesses can be found for a
procedure that remains a controversially subjective area of
the law.

All of which makes the facts surrounding a case in
Milwaukee in 1855 all the more remarkable, for in this
instance not one but ten thoroughly 'reliable' witnesses
were prepared to say 'yes' when asked the vital question.

This curious story began on the riverbank below one of
Milwaukee's bridges on 14 April 1855, when, amid a raft of
flotsam at the water's edge, a boy spied what he first thought
to be a bag or bundle of rags. Yet a closer inspection saw the
boy yell and take to his heels, for inside the loosely wrapped
bundle was the trunk of a human body, the head all but
severed and the brains dashed out by a blow on the back of

the skull. There was a great gash in the throat, the left eye protruded and both legs had been chopped off, never to be found. Importantly, though, the facial features were largely unscathed.

The Milwaukee police wasted no time in seeking identification of the body. A concentration on persons known to be missing for some time was a sound starting point. It paid dividends, for one name bandied about was that of John Dwire, a well-known face among Milwaukee's residents whom no one could recall having seen for some weeks.

Witnesses were brought forward and the police got the result they wanted as a mass of testimony confirmed the body to be that of John Dwire. All who spoke did so with the utmost assurance. They recognised his face, his features, the colour of his hair and his eyes. There, too, was the 'five-pointed starry scar' on his left cheek, the two missing front teeth, the familiar mutton-chop whiskers, the scars on the finger of the left hand and the thumb of the right. Feature after feature was identified as Dwire's as people who had known him for years nodded sagely as they examined the gruesome remains. First his landlady, then his workmates and finally the owner of the boarding house where he habitually took his meals. Ten sound witnesses provided as positive an identification as it was possible to get.

Yet, even while the inquest before which these statements were made was proceeding, rumours began to circulate that other acquaintances of Dwire's had come forward to say he was alive and well and living upriver, just 16 miles (25.7km) away: 'He's been up at Kemper's Pier for several months, since Christmas in fact,' they said.

The police were sceptical and those who had identified Dwire knew these latest reports must be bogus. The sightings, obviously, were cases of mistaken identity. Nevertheless, the police sent a delegation to Kemper's Pier to look for the 'dead' man but their journey drew a blank.

Yet back at the inquest events took a conclusive turn, for while they were on their way upriver a new witness appeared at the courthouse to weigh in with his own positive identification. We've all seen those Agatha Christie stage plays where the audience gasps in the third act. Well, the 'Case of the Unexpected Witness' was a gasper and a half and all present were dumbfounded as the eleventh man delivered his sworn statement: 'Lest anyone here should still think I'm dead I have come in person to assure him that I am not the corpse found in the river last Saturday morning.'

The body was never positively identified, nor was the murderer caught. And the ten most unreliable witnesses in legal history must have been sorely embarrassed as John Dwire achieved instant celebrity status as the only man ever to give evidence at his own inquest.

BAR TALK
DUBLIN, IRELAND, 1860

'Words are a lawyer's tools of trade.' A wise observation from that great legal luminary Lord Denning (1899–1999).

But many a barrister keen to demonstrate a mastery of words has over-egged the pudding to their cost. For every brilliant winning speech from the bar there have been countless losing ones where the question of length, in particular, has done as much damage to a defendant's cause as any amount of damning evidence.

Judge Barrington Black once mischievously marked the card of such bar bores in a tellingly brief missive to *The Times* on 9 March 1999:

> Sir, the new television series of *Kavanagh QC* is so true to life that I fell asleep during the last ten minutes of counsel's speech to the jury.

In defence of the windbags it must be said that legal history is full of genuinely stirring long speeches. Indeed entire books have been written in celebration of such gems. But brevity, just as it is said to be the soul of wit, also lies at the heart of many examples of classic advocacy, which is, in its purest form, merely the art of saying the right thing in the right way at the right time.

It's for that very reason that a short speech made in 1860 by an Irish lawyer during a very workaday case is even today quoted in full as an example of its art. Odd that it should have survived into its third century, but if a nail was ever to be hit on its head then a counsel by the name of Dr Webb was surely the man to wield the hammer to best effect.

He was appearing before the Recorder of Dublin for Peter Mulligan, a respectable young man of 25, who was applying for a licence for a public house in the fair city. The police objected on the grounds of the applicant's youth and the learned recorder echoed that view, stating gravely to Webb, 'He is very young for such a responsible position.'

It was then that Dr Webb earned his fee in a memorable manner: 'My Lord,' he said, 'Alexander the Great at 22 years of age had crushed the Illyrians and razed the city of Thebes to the ground, had crossed the Hellespont at the head of his army, had conquered Darius with a force of one million in the defiles of Issus and brought the great Persian empire under his sway. At 23, Réne Descartes evolved a new system of philosophy. At 24, Pitt was Prime Minister of the British Empire, on which the sun never sets. At 24, Napoleon overthrew his enemies with a whiff of grapeshot in the streets of Paris. Is it now to be judicially decided that Peter Mulligan, at the age of 25, is too young to manage a public house in Capel Street?'

One eminent barrister once took 17 days to deliver his final speech and still lost his case. Dr Webb took no more than 45 seconds to deliver his. Little surprise that he was later raised to the bench and became County Court Judge for Donegal. Little surprise, too, that pints were raised in his honour at the grand opening of 'Mulligan's Bar'.

SWEET FANNY ADAMS
ALTON, HAMPSHIRE, 1867

Only a very singular case could bestow on the English language a phrase still in everyday use well over a century after the event that gave birth to it. This is a singular case indeed.

'Sweet Fanny Adams', 'Sweet FA' or 'Sweet ...' you know what. Whichever strength of the well-known phrase one elects to use, the meaning amounts to the same – 'not much at all' or 'nothing of any consequence'. What a dreadful tale those words allude to.

Fanny Adams was a pretty village girl with long blonde hair and bright blue eyes, just seven years old, living in the village of Alton, near Winchester, Hampshire. 'The village stood on the Pilgrim's Way,' a tourist guidebook tells us, 'and in summer the fields hereabouts are green with trailing hops to supply Alton's breweries.' It is a description that conjures up the quintessential English scene of idyllic long hot summers, and it was just such a scene in Alton in the summer of 1867. But the guidebook does not tell us what happened on the afternoon of Saturday, 24 August.

A solicitor's clerk, Frederick Baker, saw no point in being cooped up in the office all Saturday, so he used his tea break to good advantage, strolling out into the meadows near the hop fields by the River Wey.

Fanny Adams and her two friends were playing happily when Baker passed them. He gave them half-pennies to run races for him and then sent two of the girls home while he took Fanny into the hop field, later stopping off for a beer at the Swan Inn before returning to his office.

After Fanny was reported missing the horrified villagers found the body. Baker was arrested and at the inquest in the Duke's Head Inn three days later the jury viewed the body and heard the gruesome details of the discovery of the dismembered corpse.

The severed head was stuck on the top of a hop pole with the eyes gouged out and one ear torn off; the upper torso, cut off at the diaphragm, had the heart scooped out, left on the ground nearby; each arm was deposited separately, with two half-pennies still being clutched in one hand; one foot was discovered in a field of clover; both eyes were found in the River Wey; the legs were assumed to have been taken by the river's current; there was no evidence of a sexual assault because the lower abdomen was never found.

All the evidence suggested Baker had battered the poor child with a large stone and then butchered her with his penknife. He was unable to explain bloodstains on his cuffs and his main defence, that his knife was too small to have done the damage, was weak.

That any man should have behaved in such a way was an abomination and that Baker was a man who worked in the business of law seemed only to make it worse. Under magisterial examination at Winchester Town Hall on Thursday, 29 August, he strongly protested his innocence and asked for more time to prepare for calling a fellow clerk, Mr French, as a witness. The extra time was granted, but to no avail. Baker was found guilty of wilful murder and was hanged at Winchester at 8a.m. on Christmas Eve 1867 before a high-spirited crowd of 5,000.

His case had not been helped by the discovery of his diary in the drawer of his desk. The final entry for Saturday, 24 August, read: 'Killed a young girl. It was fine and hot.'

That so little was left of sweet Fanny Adams's body lends

graphic meaning to the phrase we now use. It explains, too, why 'Fanny Adams' became navy slang for the canned mutton first introduced into sailors' rations in 1869 and why the term was used as a generic name for meat stew as late as the 1940s.

Those who say the world today is cruel are right. But there are also those who say, after the latest child abduction makes the tabloid headlines, 'It never used to happen in the old days; children had freedom and fun back then; now they've got sweet FA.'

If only they knew what they were saying. Make no mistake – child murder is as old as the hills. Even in the hop fields of Alton in that golden summer of 1867, there was evil under the sun.

THE VOICE OF CONSCIENCE

NORWICH, 1869

Like the little boy who runs to his mother to say, 'It wasn't me who broke the vase' – even before his dastardly crime has been discovered – criminals of a rather more serious breed have long suffered the seemingly unbearable torture of the guilt complex, which makes remaining undetected almost as much of an ordeal as getting caught.

Police know from experience that the urge to place the blame elsewhere, to revisit the crime scene or to make a confession is a strong one indeed and many criminals would have remained undetected but for succumbing to one of these strangely seductive and often overwhelming desires.

One of the oddest cases of this type is that of the 'Norwich Murderer' William Sheward who had so completely got away with killing his wife that he had nothing to fear whatsoever. Yet so badly did the incident play on his mind that he eventually issued a full confession to a startled police officer. Odd that he should do so at all – but even odder that he should wait fully 18 years to spill the beans.

It was in June 1851 that the Norwich tailor William Sheward, living with his older wife Martha in a somewhat strained relationship, committed the crime that was to haunt him. After what he later described as 'a violent altercation about money matters', he attacked his wife with a razor and slit her throat. Having then gone out drinking, he spent the night in the house with his wife's corpse before embarking next morning on the painstaking and gruesome disposal of evidence.

It took him five days to complete a full dismemberment and the resulting body parts were either thrown down sewers or buried at various locations in the suburbs.

When Martha Sheward was missed he told friends and relations she had left him for another man in London and he had no idea where they were. Some of Martha's relations felt this to be out of character and suggested to police that they investigate, but when they interviewed Sheward they were more than satisfied with his story, regarding him as nothing more than a mild, inoffensive, if somewhat weak, creature.

Nasty moment number one was over for Sheward but far worse looked set to come when an inquisitive dog out for walkies in Lakenham, a suburb of Norwich, discovered a hand and then a foot loosely buried in undergrowth. Over the next few days Norwich police discovered many more body parts in the vicinity and were able to reconstruct an approximation of an entire corpse, which William Sheward knew only too well to be that of his 55-year-old wife.

The outcome of the investigation depended on forensic evidence, not nearly as scientific in the Victorian era as it is now, and a police surgeon got it spectacularly wrong: 'The well-filled understructures of the skin,' he wrote, 'its delicacy and the neatness of the foot, the clean well-trimmed nails of both hands and feet, suggest a person not accustomed to toil and aged between 16 and 26.'

That truly stunning own goal led police to accept that the body parts were those of 'a missing young person unknown' and with that erroneous verdict Martha Sheward was assumed to be just one of many women drawn to the metropolis in search of a better life. William Sheward was off the hook for the second time.

Left with his own guilt and conscience he must have had a scare two years later when police again knocked at his door asking after Martha Sheward, but all it was on this occasion was that she had been left a £300 inheritance and needed to claim it in person. Again William Sheward said she was 'somewhere in London'. With this third and final let-off the case was as good as closed.

The Norwich tailor continued his trade, remarried and had two sons. Yet friends said he seemed unsettled. He suffered bouts of depression, took to heavy drinking and talked of leaving Norwich for good. And that he did, moving to London, where he was led seemingly by irresistible forces to Walworth, the very spot where he had first made acquaintance with his murdered wife.

It was 1869 when his conscience could stand no more and he resolved to commit suicide – 'but the Almighty would not let me do it,' he later told police.

That left only one way of escape from his tortured world. Confession. He duly made a full statement to police, who at first discarded it as the ramblings of a crank, but, when the case was reopened and the same police surgeon was interviewed again about the certainty of his deductions, they accepted that the mystery remains must indeed have been those of Martha Sheward.

Fully 18 years after his crime, William Sheward was tried for murder, found guilty and hanged at Norwich in 1869. He had been betrayed by nothing but his own conscience.

This cautionary case should be a lesson to us all. Unless we are prepared to spend a lifetime racked by guilt, assailed by doubt and in danger of breaking the Olympic high-jump record each time the doorbell rings, it pays to leave wife-murdering to those with a touch more bottle than poor William Sheward.

MAN'S BEST FRIEND?
COUNTY CORK, IRELAND, 1883

'Is there any other point to which you would wish to draw my attention?'
'To the curious incident of the dog in the night-time.'
'The dog did nothing in the night-time.'
'That was the curious incident,' remarked Sherlock Holmes.

That dialogue between Inspector Gregory and the world's greatest consulting detective is from the short story 'The Adventure of Silver Blaze', first published in 1892. Holmes's lateral thinking led him to believe that the dog of the household must have known the intruder on his master's premises.

One wonders if Holmes's creator Arthur Conan Doyle had half a mind on turning on its head a real case from just a few years earlier. For in 1883 a dog named Sam gave evidence of a singular kind which left a couple of violent housebreakers feeling more than a little betrayed. The game is afoot.

Elderly widow Mrs Fitzgerald lived with her daughters in a house at the foot of Mushera Mountain in County Cork. One of the less welcome legacies of her late husband was an agrarian dispute with members of the Twohey family who, even in the face of Mr Fitzgerald's death, were not prepared to let the matter lie. Two brothers of the family, Jeremiah and James Twohey, broke into the Fitzgerald home, threatened and assaulted the old lady and beat up her daughters. It was a violent and cowardly act but they looked like getting away with it.

They were charged on the evidence of an informer, at that time termed an 'approver', named Connell, but to make the charge stick the law in Ireland in those days required corroborative evidence from an independent source. Connell gave full details of the Twohey brothers' preparation for and participation in the raid, but no further evidence was forthcoming.

Mother and daughters were too shaken to identify their assailants with confidence and in any case suspected they may have been in disguise. There was a servant who seemed prepared to identify the Twohey brothers, but that evidence was thought by police to be too shaky to lead to a conviction.

Leading the prosecution at the court case in Cork in 1883 was to be Peter O'Brien, then a Senior Crown Prosecutor, but later to be Lord Chief Justice of Ireland. Even his burgeoning advocacy skills looked set to struggle to bring the case home against the Twohey boys. Nor was he yet practised enough to bring to bear the shrewd but rather naughty jury-packing tactics that he was later so notorious for trying in an effort to secure cast-iron convictions – tactics that earned him the famous nickname 'Peter the Packer'.

Peter O'Brien looked like needing help, and he got it from an unusual source. When police had attended the scene of the crime they found a dog wandering close to the premises, seemingly lost. It didn't belong to the Fitzgeralds and when it was taken to the police station no one claimed it. Before the trial, on the hunch that the mystery pooch may have been left behind by the assailants as they fled the scene of the crime, Sub-Inspector Starkie and his sidekick Captain Plunkett bundled it into a sack and released it within sniffing distance of the Twohey brothers' home.

The results would have been most gratifying even to

the great Sherlock Holmes. Sam, the unwitting canine informant left behind by his owners as they scarpered, did what came naturally and made straight for the Twohey household.

There the entire family made great efforts to shoo him away, but Sam was pleased to be home and greeted his owners in the time-honoured fashion of a faithful friend, wagging his tail furiously and reserving particular affection for his master, James Twohey. Sam's reaction might not have been admissible evidence in its own right but, when a search of the Twohey household revealed disguises and hidden ammunition, the vital independent supporting evidence was in place.

At the subsequent trial both prisoners were found guilty and Peter O'Brien made sure Sam was present in court to help press home his prosecution, where again the dog recognised the prisoners without needing a second glance.

Many is the time in history when dogs have protected their masters, sniffed out bodies or led police, Lassie-style, to hidden booty or badly injured victims. That's why they're called 'man's best friend' and why an old Irish proverb says, 'The dog that's always on the go is better than the one that's always asleep.'

Try selling those old chestnuts to the Twohey brothers. Instinctively betrayed by the heroic Sam, they each got seven years' penal servitude.

THERE'S ALWAYS PARKER
THE HIGH COURT, LONDON, 1884

The Queen v. Dudley and Stephens was one of the strangest cases in Victoria's reign, which is saying something for an age in which bizarre occurrences were seemingly two a penny.

It is one of those rare cases that beg the question, 'What would you have done?' It's a tough one to call.

The tale begins with the shipwreck on 5 July 1884 of the yacht *Mignonette* in the South Atlantic nearly 2,000 miles (3,219km) from land on a journey from England to Australia.

Blessedly there were survivors. Three men, Captain Thomas Dudley, Edwin Stephens and Ned Brooks, were able to take to a small open boat. With them was 17-year-old Parker the cabin boy, whose parents had taken the sensible precaution to name him Richard rather than Roger.

Without food or fresh water the foursome drifted for 18 days, managing to catch and consume just one small turtle in that time. As hunger raged and minds became distorted, the survival instinct kicked in.

Dudley and Stephens suggested to Brooks that one of their number should be sacrificed for food, for all four would surely perish otherwise. Their intentions were all too clear. A kill, then cannibalism. Parker, undeniably a boy of tender years, was ominously left out of the debate.

Brooks made it clear he was repulsed by the idea and would have nothing to do with it, but, by day 20, Dudley and

Stephens could hold out no longer. They resolved to eat and their menu plan had Parker on every course.

Dudley did the deadly deed, ably assisted by Stephens. The weak and defenceless cabin boy was slaughtered in cold blood and duly ripped apart. Over the next four days they ate his flesh and drank his blood. And that included Brooks, who, once the murder was done, seemed to acquire a sudden taste for the P-plan diet.

Their survival instincts paid off, as they were rescued on the twenty-fourth day by a passing German barque, the *Montezuma*, which brought them to Falmouth. When their grisly story unfolded the three survivors were surprisingly embraced by the public as heroes, and when it became clear there must be a trial there was a widespread popular clamour for their acquittal, which those on the other side of the law, undoubtedly thinking of Parker, found extremely hard to swallow.

The case was first heard before Judge Baron Huddleston at Exeter Assizes on 6 November 1884. The judge was so anxious to secure convictions that he took the unusual step of directing the jury to deliver a 'special verdict', which permitted them merely to state what they perceived as the true facts of the case, relieving them of the onerous responsibility of delivering an ultimate verdict. 'Upon the matter of the prisoners being guilty,' Judge Huddleston announced in his summing up, 'the jury are entirely ignorant. I therefore refer it to a higher court.'

When the case was heard before the five judges of the Queen's Bench Division of the High Court of Justice in London, the central question was whether Dudley and Stephens were guilty of murder or whether, on a legal technicality, the doctrine of necessity overrode that verdict. Brooks, by the way – although morally culpable of a rather shameful duplicity – was not charged with murder.

Lord Coleridge presided amid huge media interest. The defence argued that four human lives would have been lost but for the act. Being the weakest, Parker would surely have gone first and the taking of his life merely pre-empted what appeared to be inevitable by natural causes. In a long summing up Lord Coleridge was sympathetic and conceded that 'these men were subject to a terrible temptation and to sufferings which might break down the bodily power of the strongest man and try the conscience of the best'.

Yet he was unable to reconcile the facts completely and finished without ambiguity: 'It is therefore our duty to declare that the prisoners' act was wilful murder and that the facts stated are no legal justification for what they did.'

Lord Coleridge duly passed the death sentence on Dudley and Stephens but reserved more sympathy for them than he would ever have accorded to common murderers by suggesting that 'the Crown may wish to consider the possibility of a pardon in such extraordinary circumstances'.

It was indeed a supreme irony that, having fought so desperately to preserve their lives, the men should then face losing them at a stroke. After due consideration the Crown did show mercy. The death sentences were commuted to just six months' imprisonment without hard labour.

This truly extraordinary case starkly divided opinions. Who can say with any certainty how they would have reacted adrift on the high seas? Starvation or Parker? An indigestible question indeed.

THREE-TIMES-LUCKY LEE

EXETER, 1885

During the early hours of 15 November 1884 Miss Emma Keyse was brutally murdered at her pretty thatched cottage in Babbacombe, near Torquay. The local community was outraged, for Miss Keyse, a former lady-in-waiting to Queen Victoria, was a wealthy and much-respected elderly spinster who lived a blameless life.

The police investigation quickly identified 20-year-old footman John Lee as the prime suspect. He had argued with Miss Keyse over household discipline, his duties and wages and had apparently cut her throat and battered her head at the dead of night in a cold-blooded act of revenge.

Lee was arrested and committed to trial at Exeter. Proceedings began on 2 February 1885 but in three days it was all up. The prosecution case was overwhelming and the jury took only 40 minutes to find the prisoner guilty of murder.

As Mr Justice Manisty passed the inevitable sentence of death, he remarked on Lee's curiously calm and collected demeanour during the trial and suggested he spend his few remaining days alive in preparation for the next world. The condemned man's reply has entered legal history as the most prophetic of all time: 'The reason, my lord, why I am so calm and collected is because I trust in my Lord, and he knows I am innocent.'

Such bravado in the face of certain death was by no means

unusual and Lee was removed from the courtroom and taken back to Exeter Prison. He remained in a condemned cell until 23 February when the sentence was to be carried out. His execution was to be by the infallible long-drop method of hanging – once the trapdoors opened and the body plummeted down, a broken neck and instant death was a medical certainty. A few lucky men and women had survived the old-fashioned, non-scientific hangings that had preceded the new method but the long-drop had been 100 per cent effective. Survival was impossible.

In the face of that, Lee's faith in God seemed naively misplaced, and his claim to have had a dream on the eve of his execution in which he survived three attempts to hang him was dismissed as nothing but desperate wishful thinking.

The executioner James Berry wasn't interested in Lee's dreams. He was preoccupied checking and testing the trapdoor mechanism above the 11-ft (3.4-m) deep pit in the prison coach house. He found everything in perfect working order.

Just before eight o'clock on the morning of 23 February, John Lee was led to the place of execution, his legs were strapped together, the rope was placed around his neck and a white cap pulled down over his face. Ten newspaper reporters watched as Lee remained impassive while a chaplain concluded the burial service. As the chaplain finished, James Berry pulled the lever to open the double trapdoor through which John Lee would hurtle to his death.

But an astonishing thing happened. *Nothing* happened. Despite Berry's continued movement of the lever to and fro the trapdoors remained firmly closed.

The noose and cap were removed from Lee's head and he was moved forward while emergency repairs were effected with an axe, a saw and a plane. The apparatus was then tested and found to be working perfectly. Once again Lee was put in position and Berry pulled the lever. But again to the astonishment of all present, the trapdoors stayed firmly closed. This was new territory for Hangman Berry and the prison officials, but after frantic discussions they determined to go for another attempt. Again they tested the apparatus. Again it worked. Again Lee was led forward. Again he survived despite Berry's stamping furiously on the trapdoors as he pulled the lever on this third attempt to hang John Lee.

As all present looked on dumbfounded it was the prison chaplain, the Reverend John Pitkin, whose presence of mind then called the shots. He wrote in his memoirs that 'we were all mentally paralysed by the hopelessness of the task we were by law expected to perform. Three times I had concluded the service and I announced that I would remain at the place of execution no longer.'

In that way Lee was saved from death by the act of a man of God, for further attempts to dispatch him could not legally be made without the chaplain's participation.

Lee was taken back to his cell and large crowds gathered outside Exeter Prison when the news of his three-time survival was broken. Although the prison authorities were determined to try again, and indeed Lee himself encouraged them to do so, public opinion clamoured for the prisoner's death sentence to be lifted.

That same afternoon the Home Secretary William Harcourt put Lee's sentence on hold and it was later commuted to life imprisonment. While waiting for the news, Lee wrote to his sister asserting that his survival was 'a miracle worked by the Lord'.

After a detailed investigation of this strange affair the prison authorities suggested that damp conditions had caused the trapdoors to swell and wedge together when Lee's weight was applied to them.

Whatever the reason, the failure of the mechanism permitted John Lee to spend 22 years in Portland Prison, Dorset, which he had never expected. He was released on

17 December 1907 and went back to live with his widowed mother in the village of Abbotskerswell, Devon. Many members of the public, in particular the victim's relations, were outraged that he had been allowed to survive at all. Equally large numbers thought he deserved his luck and great interest was aroused when *Lloyd's Weekly News* serialised his life story.

Lee further capitalised on this interest by having the story published in book form as *The Man They Could Not Hang*, making enough money from this to live very comfortably for some months. A year after his release from Portland Prison he married, moved to London and subsequently fathered two children. Although he worked as a humble barman his celebrity was perpetuated when a silent film based on his life was shown around the country to enthusiastic audiences.

His later life is shrouded in mystery but he is generally believed to have split from his wife and travelled, dying aged 68 in Milwaukee, USA, in 1933. What is certain is that John Lee lived nearly 50 years of extra life because of nothing more than gremlins in the works. His astonishing survival of the hangman's noose remains the most remarkable case of its type of all time.

A SHOCKING AFFAIR
NEW YORK, UNITED STATES, 1890

When William Kemmler, of Buffalo, New York, took a hatchet to his mistress, Tillie Zeigler, on 29 March 1889, he might well have known that the brutal murder would lead him to the courtroom.

But that he would be immortalised as a result of the verdict was not what he had in mind. The reason for his fame is clear, though, for William Kemmler was the first ever person to be condemned to death by the electric chair. And it didn't go well.

When the jury found him guilty of murder they marked a historic moment in legal history, the moment the barbaric, unreliable and primeval practice of hanging was swept aside in America for something quicker, cleaner and far more humane, something more befitting of a civilised nation that embraced new technology and recognised human dignity. That's the theory, but it proved a tougher cookie than the Americans had bargained for.

Even before the conviction strange forces were at work, for Kemmler's defence was sponsored ... by an electricity company. There was method in this apparently distasteful madness, for the electrocution, if it happened, was set to take place using the Westinghouse Electric Company's newfangled Alternating Current. This was being promoted by them as a cheaper and safer form of electricity supply than the direct-current system pioneered by Thomas

Edison, and the idea that it could kill in an instant wasn't at all good for the ad campaign. The Westinghouse Company wanted to get Kemmler off, guilty or not.

They didn't, and Kemmler's execution was set for 6 August 1890 at New York's Auburn Prison. The death chamber was a large room with viewing seats provided for officials and reporters. Kemmler was led in and introduced by the warden in the manner of a master of ceremonies. This was theatre.

After a short speech Kemmler removed his coat and was strapped into the wooden chair before electrodes were secured in place by Deputy Sheriff Joseph Veiling, one on his head and another on his back. Kemmler's last words were to the point: 'Don't get excited, Joe, I want you to make a good job of this.'

On a signal from the warden, the executioner, hidden from view in an adjoining room, threw the switch and for fully 17 seconds 1,000 volts pulsed through Kemmler's body, which contorted and strained, eyes bulging, as the current did its deadly job. When it was all over doctors gathered round the chair to confirm the deed was done as reporters looked on. The next day's *New York World* described what followed:

Suddenly the breast heaved. There was a straining on the straps. The man was alive! Everybody lost their wits and someone gave a startled cry for the current to be switched on again. The handle could be heard as it was pulled back and forth time and again to break the deadly current into jets.

They let it run this time for four minutes before the prisoner was finally pronounced dead. Although Kemmler had been unconscious throughout the ordeal it was accepted that it was a bungled operation and most of the press described it as 'horrific'. Only the *New York Times* stuck their neck out by saying, 'It would be absurd to talk of abandoning the law and going back to the barbarism of hanging.'

They were proved right, for voltages were subsequently increased and the electric chair flourished, although even as late as 1983 it still took nearly ten minutes to finish off John Evans in Alabama's Holman Prison. Meanwhile, the worst fears of the Westinghouse Electricity Company over negative publicity were unfounded, for they and their new system also went from strength to strength.

There is a humorous postscript to the unsavoury case of William Kemmler. Later in 1890, as news of the ongoing use of the electric chair spread worldwide, Emperor Menlek II of Abyssinia (now Ethiopia) was so impressed by stories of its efficiency that he ordered three from New York. He had over-looked one vital factor though. Abyssinia had no electricity!

Two of the chairs were promptly thrown out and he used the third as a throne, so Emperor Menlek is one of just a handful of men to have sat in the electric chair and lived to tell the tale.

A UNIQUE DISCOVERY
NECHOCHEA, ARGENTINA, 1892

The quality of strangeness, particularly in relation to the scientific techniques of criminology, is one that shifts with time, for by today's standards the capture and conviction of a murderess in the province of Buenos Aires, Argentina, in July 1892, was tediously routine.

Yet, at the time, the methods used to incriminate the culprit were as 'cutting-edge' as any of the myriad computer-aided techniques now increasingly applied. It is odd that the small town of Nechochea should have secured a permanent place in legal history, but then the first ever use of fingerprints in a successful detection is certainly something worth shouting about, bearing in mind the subsequent use of that method in bringing millions of criminals to justice.

The build-up to this celebrated case is interesting because the concept of fingerprints had been talked about long before their use in a real situation. A Scots-born doctor and teacher, Henry Faulds, submitted a short monograph on the uniqueness of this human 'calling card' and its potential use in catching criminals to the magazine *Nature* and it was published on 28 October 1880. Alas, the British authorities took little notice of his 'cranky' views, and, just eight years later in London, a certain Jack the Ripper was able to leave his prints all over the place without ever being caught.

Even writers of fiction were more ahead of the game than police. American author Mark Twain mentioned thumbprinting criminals in his 1883 *Life On the Mississippi*, and two years before that, in the December 1881 edition of *Chambers' Journal*, a ripping yarn entitled 'The Story of a Thumb-Mark' described how a murderer was caught by use of Henry Faulds's recently publicised technique.

It was only a matter of time before science fiction became science fact and the unlucky first victim of this advance was Francesca Rojas. When her two young children were found with their throats cut Francesca was also found to have a superficial throat wound and she laid the blame for the murders and 'attempted murder' firmly at the door of her neighbour Velasquez.

He was arrested and questioned but police were unsure of his guilt and wrote to the police Bureau of Anthropometric Identification in La Plata for help. In charge of the bureau was Juan Vucetich, an enthusiast of the Faulds methods, and he instructed his colleague Inspector Edward Alvarez to make a detailed examination of the crime scene.

When Alvarez found bloody fingerprints on a door jamb he sawed out the relevant section and sent it back to Vucetich with sample prints taken from the mother and suspect. The prints were quickly shown to belong to the mother and, since she had denied ever touching the children after she had supposedly 'found' them dead, it was certain she was lying. When confronted with the scientific 'proof' she broke down, offered a full confession and was duly tried, found guilty and given a lengthy prison term.

Vucetich had undeniably triumphed in making a major breakthrough and as a consequence he started the world's first fingerprinting bureau to put Argentina at the forefront of new detection techniques.

Yet the strangest postscript to the pioneering Francesca Rojas case is how slow other forces were to cotton on and how it was the lesser-developed nations who were first to react.

Outside Argentina the first use of fingerprints in a murder

case was in Bengal, India, in May 1898, when a thief called Kangali Charan was charged with murdering his former employee.

Again prints linked him inextricably with the theft and murder, but the Indian court, evidently wary of the power of this new technology, perversely saw fit to find him guilty only of the theft.

It wasn't until the conviction of Henri Scheffer on 14 March 1903 for murdering a dentist's manservant in Paris that prints were used in a capital case in Europe, and it was fully 25 years after Henry Faulds's 'cranky' monograph, that a British murderer was finally convicted on fingerprint evidence.

Maybe Scotland Yard were making up for lost time, for at the Old Bailey on 23 May 1905 the Stratton brothers were found guilty of the double murder of an elderly man and his wife at their chandler's shop in Deptford High Street, south London.

Now we have DNA profiling and sophisticated computer-aided analysis of voice, facial characteristics, handwriting and personality. But the thanks for setting the ball rolling goes to the Scottish scientist and Argentinian police chief so willing to stick their necks out over a century ago.

IN THE FOOTSTEPS
OF SWEENEY TODD
CHICAGO, UNITED STATES, 1897

The People's Periodical and Family Library, published in
Fleet Street, London, began to sell particularly well from
November 1846. For in that issue of the 'penny dreadful' a
serial entitled *The String of Pearls* first introduced readers
to the fascinatingly macabre character of Sweeney Todd,
the 'Demon Barber of Fleet Street'.

The barber who would regularly dispatch his customers
from the chair through a trapdoor into a subterranean
morgue, after using his cutthroat razor exactly as the name
implies, provided a storyline likely to do the next issue's
sales figures no harm at all; that the hapless victims were
then butchered and ended up in the famously 'tasty pies'
sold by Mrs Lovett in her shop at Bell Yard was enough
to create record sales of *The People's Periodical* for the
18 issues in which Sweeney appeared. Pie sales, however,
dipped alarmingly for the same period.

So legendary did the tale become that by the end of the
century Sweeney Todd joined Sherlock Holmes in the
psyche of many members of the general public as one of
those 'fictional' characters who truly existed.

Yet, far-fetched as his extracurricular tonsorial activity may
have been, legal history has thrown up some strange cases
of its own that come closer to Todd's dreadful deeds than
might be imagined. May I introduce the master sausage
maker Adolph Luetgert (1848–1911)?

When he emigrated from Germany to the United States in the 1870s he settled in Chicago, showing great entrepreneurial spirit and opening a sausage factory in the neighbourhood of Lakeview.

He also had a great appetite for women. When his first wife died he married Louisa Bicknese and cemented the relationship by giving her a gold ring embossed with her new initials 'LL'. But despite this loving gesture he still took mistresses and soon became bored with Louisa.

On 11 March 1897 he decided on positive action, buying 325lb (147kg) of potash and 50lb (23.7kg) of arsenic. Neither was required in the sausage-making process. After 1 May, his wife Louisa 'disappeared', and Luetgert explained to all enquirers, including her brother Diedrich, that she had gone visiting relatives in Kankakee, Illinois.

Unable to track down his sister, Diedrich Bicknese informed the police. Captain Hermann Schluetter took up the case. On 15 May, acting on information from two factory employees, he examined the contents of a 5-ft (1.5-m) deep vat which contained a pungent greasy slime. There Officer Walter Dean made the gruesome discovery of human bone fragments and a small section of gold ring. The initials 'LL' were clearly visible.

Despite Luetgert's strenuous denials, police concluded he had ground up the body and boiled it in the vat usually used for sausage meat. Witnesses spoke of suspicious behaviour and having glimpsed Louisa with Luetgert in the factory on the night she disappeared.

When Luetgert was charged the residents of Chicago were revolted by the details. Rumours spread that Louisa had been made into sausage. In truth she never was, since the factory was being refurbished and not manufacturing at that time. But Chicago butchers saw banger sales slump for many weeks after Luetgert's unsavoury deeds were revealed.

Because no further body parts were ever discovered, the

evidence remained circumstantial. It was that which saved Luetgert's skin. At the first trial, on 21 October 1897, opinion was split as to whether he should suffer the death penalty or life imprisonment.

At the second trial, on 9 February 1898, he got the benefit of the doubt, being convicted of murder but sentenced to life imprisonment on account of the 'fragmentary' evidence.

Luetgert died in the Joliet State Penitentiary in 1911, a shadow of his former self, claiming his wife was haunting him. His attorney Lawrence Harmon also suffered mental strain after losing the case. So convinced was he that Louisa would one day turn up to save the day that he spent $2,000 of his own savings searching for her. She never appeared and Harmon died insane in a mental institution.

Although the sausage factory burnt down in 1902 and was never rebuilt, Chicago folklore has it that the ghost of Louisa Luetgert still walks the site.

This case remains one of the oddest murders on record, and still without an entirely conclusive solution. Could the haunting spectre of the 'sausage lady' be the missing link?

A THEATRICAL PERFORMANCE

THE OLD BAILEY, LONDON, 1898

The similarities between a courtroom scene and the stage are legion. Elaborate costume, stirring speeches, witty asides and the serried 'audience' ranks make for everything from high drama to cruel tragedy and hilarious farce.

So when genuine thespians really do appear in court, the worlds of stage and law can become one to theatrical effect. Enter stage left Richard 'Mad Archie' Prince.

Dundee-born Prince, christened Richard Millar Archer, the son of a humble ploughman, was everything the archetypal 'wannabe' invariably is – full of ambition, full of himself, but largely devoid of talent. The eccentric Scotsman was a 'cannabe' of cringeworthy averageness – at best.

He'd reached the age of 39 scratching nothing more than a meagre living from occasional small parts, and as Christmas 1897 loomed he was 'resting' for the umpteenth time. His Actors' Benevolent Fund maintenance payment had just been stopped and he was pondering where his next decent meal would come from. He was also looking for someone to blame. Enter stage right William Terriss, a handsome and hugely popular actor-manager of the flamboyant world of Victorian theatre who was everything 'Mad Archie' aspired to.

Terriss, affectionately known as 'Breezy Bill', had tried his best to help Prince by giving him small parts but had once had him thrown out of a play for offensive remarks. Even so, when Prince's 'resting' became rather too permanent, Terriss was kind enough to give him free stage passes and the odd handout.

But none of that washed with Prince, who blamed his misfortune entirely on Terriss and planned to wreak vengeance.

On the evening of 16 December 1897 Richard Prince lurked under the awning of the famous Rules Restaurant in London's Maiden Lane, not the best place for a hungry out-of-work actor to soothe his troubled brow. The woodcock with chestnut puree looked particularly inviting.

As 50-year-old William Terriss approached the rear entrance of the Adelphi Theatre opposite, prior to his performance in the play *Secret Service*, the years of frustration finally caused Richard Prince to act as he'd never acted before. Who knows what really caused him to flip? But flip he did.

He dashed across the road and plunged a kitchen knife deep into William Terriss's back. As the hero of melodrama turned and fell, a second blow slashed his side and a third inflicted a chest wound for good measure.

Terriss got the final curtain prematurely that night, dying in the Adelphi greenroom shortly after the stabbing. The evening's performance was cancelled and elsewhere in theatre land all the stages of the West End observed a minute's silence as news of the tragedy quickly spread. Richard Prince was a leading player at last.

He made no attempt to escape, but strode up and down Maiden Lane delivering a dramatic soliloquy justifying his deed. When the police arrived he meekly gave himself up and when they later offered him food at Bow Street Police Station, he burst into tears, sobbing, 'I'm so hungry.'

Act Two of Prince's gripping performance saw the scene shift to the Old Bailey on 13 January 1898. He first answered the charge of murder with a plea of 'guilty with provocation' but changed this on the advice of his counsel to 'not guilty by reason of insanity'. This was backed up by medical evidence demonstrating his 'insane delusions' and, rather less scientifically, by his loving mother. She took to the witness box to declare loudly, 'My son is soft in the head.'

Throughout the one-day trial Richard Prince wore an Inverness cape and conducted himself in a thoroughly theatrical manner, seemingly much pleased to be centre stage at last. The jury needed only half an hour to find him 'guilty but not responsible for his actions'. He was committed to the criminal lunatic asylum at Broadmoor and speedily removed from the courtroom as he attempted to make a dramatic speech of thanks.

Thus spared from the hangman's noose, Prince was said to be much happier in the surreal world of the asylum than he had been in the real world outside. There were frequent opportunities to take meals with Napoleon Bonaparte or indulge in a game of draughts with Alexander the Great, and Prince took a keen interest in all the entertainments put on by the inmates.

Mad Archie's new company might well have performed to audiences a few short of a full house but rave reviews were guaranteed.

ELEMENTARY, MY DEAR HOLMES!

GREAT WYRLEY, STAFFORDSHIRE, 1903

At the risk of disillusioning admirers of Sherlock Holmes, the world's most brilliant detective of all time, it is my sorry duty to report that the great man never solved a single case in his life. He was a fictional character – a shock to the countless fans who have written to him at 221B Baker Street over the years. Sooner or later someone will be telling us that Santa Claus doesn't exist – it's a cruel world we live in.

Yet strangely the razor-sharp intellect and unique powers of observation we associate with Holmes did help shape the course of British justice, because his creator Sir Arthur Conan Doyle used his own considerable knowledge of the art of detection to help solve a singular crime and usher in a law that has benefited the wrongly accused for almost a century since. 'The Case of the Mutilated Beasts' might sound like one of Doyle's more far-fetched stories, but this one was for real.

In the latter years of the nineteenth century the vicar of Great Wyrley in Staffordshire was Shapurji Edalji, a Parsee Indian married to an Englishwoman, who had a son named George. The family met with considerable uncharitable xenophobia from parishioners. In 1888 a series of threatening anonymous messages were scrawled on walls around Great Wyrley parish. When a disaffected servant girl admitted writing them Edalji let the matter rest, not wishing to create a fuss.

Then between 1892 and 1895, anonymous letters in a different hand were sent to the Edaljis, and many cruel practical jokes were played on the family. Unbidden deliveries were made to their home, advertisements under the vicar's name placed in the newspapers, rubbish strewn on their lawn, and mysteriously a key from Walsall Grammar School was left on their doorstep. The local Chief Constable, the Honourable G.R. Anson, investigated the incidents and told Edalji that it was his own son George, a pupil at Malvern School, who was responsible – a 'difficult teenage phase', nothing more.

Despite George's protestations of innocence, believed by his father completely, the matter was again put to rest.

But from February to August 1903, by which time George had entered into practice as a Birmingham solicitor, Great Wyrley was again back in the news when a bizarre series of animal mutilations occurred in the parish – 16 sheep, cattle and horses had their stomachs ripped open and letters were sent to the police accusing George Edalji of being 'The Great Wyrley Beast Killer'.

He was duly arrested and put in jail to await trial. Police had found 'horse-hairs and blood' on his jacket cuffs and other circumstantial evidence, which they said linked Edalji firmly to the outrage.

George was a quiet, studious and very sensitive young man and he wrote to the press from his prison cell offering his life savings of £25 to anyone who could give a clue that would lead to the real culprit. No one came forward until a hysterical farmer's son, Harry Green, sensationally confessed to the mutilations.

The police rejected his statement and promptly ushered him from the scene by assisting his passage for an extended visit to South Africa. Edalji, meanwhile, was tried, found guilty and sent to prison for seven years late in 1903, despite the animal mutilations having continued even while he was in custody.

It was an outrageous stitch-up fuelled entirely by racial hatred – one Birmingham newspaper said the killings were 'sacrifices which were part of Edalji's elaborate Black Magic rituals'.

The police and public were happy with the conviction but a number of solicitors and barristers sent a petition to the Home Office expressing their outrage. It was ignored, although it may have contributed to Edalji's early release for good behaviour in 1906.

Once free of his prison nightmare Edalji, barred from legal practice, promptly gave his own account of the affair in a sporting magazine called *The Umpire*. Sir Arthur Conan Doyle read that account.

Doyle instinctively believed Edalji and arranged to meet him to discuss the evidence in detail, and he subsequently wrote the serialised 'Story of Mr George Edalji' in *The Daily Telegraph* in January 1907.

Using all the techniques with which he had imbued Sherlock Holmes, Doyle was able to expose the police 'evidence' as an utter sham – armed with a special dispensation from Scotland Yard he was allowed to examine the exhibits.

Edalji's clothes were indeed covered in horsehair, but only because they had been taken to the police station bundled up in a box with a horse's mane. The bloodstains on his cuffs were indeed cattle blood – splashes from a joint of rare beef Edalji had enjoyed for Sunday lunch. Blood on Edalji's razor was rust, and the hairs on it were human, not equine. The anonymous letters were written by two people jealous of Edalji's respectability. Doyle was unsuccessful in getting Edalji the compensation and retrial he pushed for because the Gladstone Commission charged with re-examining the case shamefully fudged the issue.

But Edalji's name was cleared in the eyes of the public and the Law Society readmitted him to the roll of solicitors. Such was the public support, too, for Doyle's campaign, that the widespread national criticism played a major part in leading to the creation of the Court of Criminal Appeal in 1907, which has helped to furnish justice to countless men and women ever since. In as much as Sir Arthur Conan Doyle was Sherlock Holmes, the greatest detective of all time has, after all, shaped the course of British justice and 'The Case of the Mutilated Beasts' was one of his most singular triumphs.

A MAN AHEAD OF HIS TIME

HARLESDEN, LONDON, 1905

Countless murderers throughout history have been caught and convicted because they didn't plan ahead. But Arthur Devereux knew precisely that and he aimed to get away with murder by foolproof planning of the most meticulous kind. Alas for poor Arthur, though, his forward-thinking approach proved to be the very thing that finally convinced the trial jury of his guilt and condemned him to the gallows.

Devereux was working for a chemist in Hastings when he met his future wife Beatrice there in 1896. They married two years later in Paddington, but after the birth of their first son, Stanley, they began to struggle financially. Beatrice was an accomplished musician and might well have contributed significantly to the family income but for the untimely arrival of twins, Evelyn and Lawrence, in 1903. Devereux doted on young Stanley but he resented the twins from the moment they were born.

Feeling the pressure as sole breadwinner, Arthur Devereux struggled to hold down his job and began to suffer emotionally. Attempting to improve his lot, he resorted to illegal and bizarre behaviour, first forging false references to gain a position and then posing as an American millionaire.

But these excursions into fantasy paid no dividends and by December 1904 the Devereux family were in dire straits. That month they moved into a top-floor flat in Harlesden, northwest London, under the assumed name of Egerton, by which time Arthur Devereux had already decided to rid himself of the main drain on his resources, his wife and the twins. The catalyst for the dreadful deed surely occurred on 2 January 1905, when Arthur was released from his post as a chemist's assistant in Kilburn. Mrs Devereux and the twins were last seen alive on 28 January.

Although Arthur told neighbours and the milkman that they had gone to Plymouth for a rest cure, Beatrice Devereux's mother proved tougher to convince and her tip-off to the police ultimately led them to a trunk deposited in a warehouse by Devereux. It was opened on 13 April and found not to contain the bottles of chemicals that Devereux had insisted it did. Instead, tightly crammed inside the trunk, were the bodies of Beatrice Devereux and her 20-month-old twins, both still wearing their nightgowns.

Devereux was picked up by police at his new place of work in Coventry and charged with murder, to which the 34-year-old pleaded not guilty at his trial in June. The jury seemed to have a simple task, but Devereux concocted an elaborate story that might have sown the seeds of doubt in the minds of the more susceptible members of the panel.

His version was that on the morning of 28 January he had argued with his wife, taken young Stanley out for the day and returned to find his wife and twins dead in bed smelling of chloroform. It was a clear case of suicide, he said, and only the fear that suspicion would fall on him had led him first to pack the trunk with its gruesome cargo, then to pack Stanley off to boarding school in Kenilworth and finally to pack himself off to a new life in Coventry close to Stanley's school.

It might have washed with the jury but for Devereux's peculiar brand of forward planning, for he had 'imagined' the deed done before it actually occurred.

The jury began seriously to wonder when they heard the landlord of the Harlesden flat testify that Devereux said he would 'only need it for six weeks', but the clincher was

Devereux's reply to a job advertisement, which he sent off on 13 January, a full 15 days before his wife's death.

It proved to be unlucky 13 for Devereux, for in his letter he described himself as 'a widower'. It is a fatal trait in many walks of life to glimpse the winning post too early and Devereux's wishful thinking proved his final undoing. Having unwittingly proclaimed himself a murderer ahead of his time, he was pronounced guilty by the jury after ten minutes' consultation.

As an object lesson in forward planning the case of Arthur Devereux is best treated with caution by anyone intent on murder. One word out of place had cost him his life. He was hanged at Pentonville Prison on 15 August 1905.

MURDER BY REQUEST

GUILDFORD ASSIZES, 1919

It is unusual for a man to stand up in court, openly admit to stabbing someone to death, yet still expect to be found not guilty. Yet this was the scenario at Guildford Assizes on Thursday, 3 July 1919, as 17-year-old William Nelson Adams described how he stabbed 60-year-old George Jones but asked the court to consider the special circumstances surrounding his apparently cold-blooded act.

George Jones had befriended young Adams, a market porter from Blackfriars, London, and given him lodgings in his home. He treated the lad to meals and drinks and, after one such excursion to a pub in Tooting on the evening of 10 June 1919, their unlikely friendship took a curious turn.

They left the pub late at night in the company of another man, Charlie Smith, and caught a tramcar to Sutton. Shortly before midnight they alighted and walked to a local park, where Adams stabbed his elderly friend six times with a shoemaker's awl, three times in the throat and three times in the chest.

Jones was later found half alive, wearing only his trousers and vest, with his shirt wrapped awkwardly about his chest and neck as if someone had tried to stem the flow of blood. He lived for three more days and was able to tell police that he had no idea why Adams had attacked him: 'I had done nothing to him,' he said.

When Adams was arrested he told police a different story

altogether, one that he repeated in court, and one that gave the jury a dilemma that no jury had ever encountered before. Adams made no effort to deny the killing, but explained that Jones had made a request that he should perform a special service in gratitude for his kindness: 'During the tramcar journey he gave me the weapon,' Adams explained. 'He said to me, "I've done you a good turn, now you do one for me. Will you kill me?"'

This curious affair became known as the 'Murder by Request' case and Adams related to the court in detail how Jones had told him he was worried out of his life because of an income tax bill he couldn't pay.

'When we got to the park,' said Adams, 'George said to me "The best way is to stab me in the left side of the neck." I hesitated for a quarter of an hour but at last had the temptation to do it.'

The court was told that Charlie Smith, a man never found by police, watched the whole scene but did not participate. Although Adams told the court that he tried to stem the flow of blood, his cause wasn't helped by the fact that he had stolen Jones's money after the crime and fled the scene.

The jury retired after hearing Adams's final cry for mercy that he had 'only been trying to oblige the old gentleman'.

No one but Adams, the missing Charlie Smith and the dead man ever knew the real truth but there was a strong feeling in the contemporary press reports that Adams's bizarre tale might well have approximated to the truth. The jury, though, undoubtedly conscious of the possibility of setting a hugely unwise precedent, found Adams guilty of murder and the 17-year-old was sentenced to death.

Adams, though, did not hang. Home Secretary Edward Shortt commuted the 'Murder by Request' prisoner's sentence to life imprisonment.

In the wake of Adams's case, a number of subsequent murderers have used the 'request' defence, most entirely without justification, but one or two have been cited as possibly genuine. Most famous of these, and proven to be true, was the South African case of a 23-year-old bodyguard, Marthinus Rossouw, who shot his boss in the head near Cape Town in March 1961. The boss, a playboy-landowner named Baron Dieter von Schauroth, had an unhappy marriage and was suspected of being involved in illegal diamond trading. He gave Rossouw a revolver and a cheque for 2,300 rand to do the deadly deed.

At the trial in 1962 Rossouw's defence again proved a spurious one but, as the baron had recently insured his life heavily, the aftermath of the crime was a bitter wrangle between his widow and the insurance company, who said that von Schauroth's death was not 'murder' but 'assisted suicide'.

There are variations on this unusual theme. Murderers have claimed to have been hypnotised, taken over by evil spirits, guided by God or instructed by aliens. Although such cases have required a closer examination of the legal implications than most, the defendants are seldom successful, although 'killing while sleepwalking', and being in a state of 'automatism' have been allowed as valid defences on rare occasions, as has murder during the course of an epileptic fit.

On balance, though, I would suggest that anyone with murder in mind should prepare to take full responsibility for their act. Even if you are begged to do it, there is only one person who will be truly 'asking for it' – and it won't be the victim.

ONCE PICKLED, FOREVER TOASTED

PAISLEY, SCOTLAND, 1928

When May McAllister was born in Cambuslang, near Glasgow, on 4 July 1898, that she would one day alter the course of legal history would have been a fantastic notion to her plain-living steelworker father James and his wife Mary.

Yet their daughter was destined to become the pivotal figure in a bizarre incident that has become one of the most famous and influential in common-law history.

May married Henry Donoghue in 1915 but life was unkind to her in the years that followed. By 1920 she had given birth to four children, three of whom died within a matter of days, and she endured a life of harsh deprivation. In 1928 she parted from Henry and moved to her brother's flat at 49 Kent Street, Glasgow. By way of a pick-me-up she arranged to meet a friend on the pleasant summer evening of Sunday, 26 August 1928, taking a tram to nearby Paisley and strolling into Mr Minchella's inviting café for a little refreshment.

After scrutinising the menu she made the decision that would write her name indelibly into the legal history books. She ordered a ginger beer to mix with her ice cream to make a soda. As she poured some of the sparkling mineral from its opaque bottle she would have been blissfully unaware that ginger beer already had a legal record of sorts, but thereby lay the rub of the tale that was to unfold.

In 1913 a Mr Bates had bought a bottle of Batey's ginger beer from a retailer. It carried more wallop than he bargained for when it exploded in his face, causing injury. He decided to sue the manufacturer but the verdict from *Bates v. Batey and Company* was that, while the manufacturer had a contract with the retailer and the retailer had a similar relationship with the consumer, there was no bridging contract between manufacturer and consumer. Bates lost his case as the missing link won the day.

That was still the status quo when May Donoghue licked her lips at Minchella's as her friend poured out the last remnants of the bottle. But they weren't the only last remnants she saw that day as the decomposed body of a long-drowned snail slithered into the glass.

Perhaps all the frustrations of May Donoghue's life came to a head at that moment. Suitably shocked and feeling physically sick, she suffered an attack of restaurant rage and vowed, like Bates before her, to sue the manufacturer.

The case dubbed the 'Battle of the Bottle' began on 4 April 1929, but the manufacturer, Stevenson, and his representatives played the *Bates v. Batey and Company* card incessantly. It took until June 1930 for the Scottish Courts to rule that the case could proceed at all. Then in November they got cold feet and reversed their decision. By this time May Donoghue was a woman with a mission and she refused to accept that her fight was over. Even two years down the line the slimy image of that sluggardly snail would keep repeating on her.

She appealed to London's Law Lords for the right to take the case forward. Speaking for Donoghue, George Morton, unlike the dregs in question, was clarity itself: 'The ginger beer was bottled and labelled by Stevenson, it bore his name and was sealed with a metal cap by him; it was the duty of Mr Stevenson to provide a system of working which would not allow snails to inhabit this bottle and to provide an efficient system of inspection of the bottles before the ginger beer was poured into them. He failed in those duties and caused harm to my client May Donoghue.'

Five Lords sat in judgment and a majority of three needed convincing for the case to go forward. In the legal equivalent of a penalty shootout, Lord Buckmaster struck first for Stevenson:

'It is ludicrous for him to be responsible to the public for every bottle which issues from the works. This appeal should be dismissed.'

Atkin stuck his neck out and got one back for Donoghue. Tomlin put Stevenson ahead by stating that to find otherwise could have 'alarming results'. Thankerton levelled for Donoghue and Lord Macmillan stepped up calm as you like to make the casting vote in Donoghue's favour.

It had taken three years to decide that the case itself could be heard but what a historic decision it was. Yet ironically the action for damages never did reach court. Perhaps it was the strain, for the beleaguered Mr Stevenson promptly died and in December 1934 an out-of-court settlement for £200 brought the case to a close. It had dragged on for six long years, but then most snail-related cases are inclined to be slow.

To May Donoghue, then a Glasgow shop assistant, the money was nice but her life thereafter was scarcely a bed of roses. She finally divorced Henry in 1945 but began to suffer mental illness and on 19 March 1958 she died in Gartloch Mental Hospital, Glasgow, aged 59. Her entire estate was just £364 18s. 8d. (£364.94).

So May Donoghue was made neither rich nor happy by her unprecedented crusade but the case of *Donoghue v. Stevenson* established the legal link between manufacturer and end-user which allowed the litigation floodgates to open. Those who have sued successfully since have May Donoghue to thank for their fortune. But the manufacturers forced to cough up might well rue the real cost of the day a wayward mollusc took to the bottle and got pickled.

May I offer a toast in ginger beer to that trailblazing snail? But do check the glass first.

A CLERICAL ERROR
CHURCH HOUSE, WESTMINSTER, LONDON, 1932

Doctors who murder their patients, bent coppers, corrupt solicitors or judges who break the law all provoke a strong sense of public disquiet. But where 'men of the cloth' are concerned, wry smiles and great hilarity of the nudge-nudge, wink-wink variety are more the order of the day. It seems a dodgy vicar is pure entertainment.

Naturally *The Law's Strangest Cases* must embrace these clerical tales. And the star of the show must be the Reverend Harold 'Jumbo' Davidson, the rector of Stiffkey in Norfolk. In 1932 he put the ecclesiastical courts in a right tizzy but the public were royally entertained by the newspaper reports of this singular affair in which the man dubbed 'the Prostitutes' Padre' was both disgraced and defrocked.

Harold Davidson descended from a long line of Protestant churchmen and after being ordained in 1902 became an assistant curate in Westminster. In 1906 he left London, opting for a quiet existence as rector of the parish of Stiffkey with Morston, a sleepy fishing community in northwest Norfolk.

But he missed the bright lights of London. Able to dispatch his Stiffkey duties in a couple of days a week, he took to staying in London for much of the time and became a tireless campaigner for every cause going, writing to MPs and influential families begging for donations for 'the less fortunate'.

Newsboys and waitresses were two of his favourite causes, only eclipsed by his 'concern' for actresses and prostitutes. Davidson became, with the full backing of the Bishop of Norwich, the accredited chaplain to the Actors' Church Union; he took to appearing backstage at West End theatres, where he was later variously remembered as 'a well-meaning innocent' and 'a voyeuristic pest' – 'Sorry, ladies, I didn't know this was your changing room', spoken in a suitably bumbling-vicar sort of way, was the kind of 'mistake' he made with startling regularity.

It was when he started taking London prostitutes back to stay at his home in Stiffkey with his wife and five children that some of the Norfolk locals got a bit twitchy. As yet there was no evidence that Davidson was 'playing around' but certain antics between the girls and local lads were considered shocking.

A serious complaint was bound to arise, and did, but not until 1931, when Davidson was late for an Armistice Day service. A Norfolk landowner promptly wrote to the Bishop of Norwich and incorporated charges of 'impropriety' in his complaint. On 2 February 1933 the *Eastern Daily Press* reported that 'complaints concerning the moral conduct of the rector of Stiffkey have been lodged'.

This quickly became an affair of national interest – Davidson was proving an embarrassment to the church and the bishop had to act. Davidson was hauled before the Church Consistory Court at the Great Hall of Church House, Westminster. His trial lasted 25 days.

The five charges included 'embracing a young woman in a Chinese restaurant', 'making improper suggestions to waitresses' and 'maintaining an immoral liaison with a "named woman" for ten years'.

Although the evidence was wishy-washy there was a lot of it. He had never been caught *in flagrante* and Davidson and his supporters claimed that none of his liaisons had been consummated. Like Prime Minister William Gladstone before him, he was simply 'committed to the idea of salvation'.

Yet many witnesses were prepared to testify before the Worshipful F. Keppel North that Davidson's behaviour was not becoming of a churchman. There was much talk of 'fondling', 'whispering' and 'brushing against', all of which lent an air of high farce to proceedings – Davidson himself added to this by doing an impromptu tap dance in the witness stand.

It was probably the photograph of Davidson, complete with dog collar, standing alongside a half-naked teenage girl that sealed his fate. Davidson insisted this was a set-up taken on the eve of the trial, when the girl walked up to him and whipped off her shawl with a photographer on hand. This was likely true, indeed some say the church authorities set it up to nail their man. Nail him it did.

Amid intense media interest Harold Davidson was found guilty on all charges on 8 July 1932. His attempted appeal was dismissed and he was duly defrocked.

There this odd affair should end but doesn't, for the famous rector of Stiffkey, described by his own son as 'mad, quite mad' and his own lawyer as 'a troublesome busybody', seemed determined to achieve even greater immortality.

Still needing to earn a living, he set himself up as a circus-style sideshow on the promenade at Blackpool; punters paid to listen to the famously defrocked cleric protesting his innocence while sitting in a barrel, from where he wrote his memoirs. Betweentimes he made a general nuisance of himself, interrupting church services and instigating law suits, or preaching from the mouth of a stuffed whale and undertaking a 35-day hunger strike 'until the church reinstates me'.

It didn't, and Davidson was arrested for 'attempted suicide', although appearing remarkably robust for a half-starved man – not surprising, as a hidden stash of food was discovered, which had sustained him during his so-called toilet breaks.

Shameless publicity stunter he may have been but the financial rewards were significant. Davidson was said to have 'raked in up to £20,000 in the mid-thirties', a huge sum for the time.

Can this story get stranger? Yes actually. Davidson's final stunt was to appear in Skegness in 1937, again protesting his innocence but this time from a cage he shared with a couple of mangy old lions. He billed himself 'Modern Daniel in the Lion's Den'.

Geriatric the lions may have been but they obviously had a macabre sense of humour because one of the beasts, Freddy, mauled the crazy cleric in an unsympathetic manner; Davidson was rescued, appropriately by a 16-year-old girl, but died of his wounds two days later on 30 July 1937.

The most famous cleric in legal history has been the subject of an opera, a number of folk songs, several biographical studies and an underground film directed by Ken Russell. The case still provokes controversy and many say he was an innocent victim of gossipmongers. His grave in the churchyard at Stiffkey is neatly tended by loyal villagers to this day.

At worst his behaviour was shockingly immoral. At best that of a harmless buffoon. But it was surely unwise. I include no further clerics in *The Law's Strangest Cases* because the rector of Stiffkey always was an impossible act to follow. Reverend, you have given lots of people lots of fun – how many clerics can we say that about?

A SELF-INFLICTED WOUND

THE HIGH COURT, LONDON, 1933

A London stockbroker, William Lewis Rowland Paul Sebastian Blennerhassett, was proud of his name. His ancestor Alan de Blenerhayset had been Mayor of Carlisle in 1382 and members of the family had been MPs for that city right from the reign of Richard II to that of James I.

He was proud too of the Distinguished Service Order awarded for his wartime conduct. Proud of serving as a delegate to the League of Nations. Proud of his 30 years as a stockbroker in Throgmorton Street. Safe to conclude that Mr Blennerhassett was a proud man. Pity he didn't remember that 'pride comes before a fall'.

He had enjoyed a pleasant lunch on 26 May 1932 but was much perturbed on his return to work to be greeted by jeers, ribald laughter and much nodding and winking. Only when he was shown that day's *Evening Standard* did he get the joke, for there was a full-page advert for the latest novelty-toy craze, the yo-yo, telling the story of a man who bought a 'Cheerio 99' for each of his two children but became obsessed by it and ended up in a mental institution. It was an amusing yarn nicely illustrated, but Mr B stared aghast at some of the copy:

Take warning by the fate of Mr Blennerhassett, as worthy a citizen as any that ever ate lobster at Pimm's or holed a putt at Walton Heath. 'Sound man, Blennerhassett', they said on Throgmorton Street. But Yo-Yo got him and today he is happy in a quiet place in the country under sympathetic surveillance as he practises Yo-Yo tricks. So beware of Yo-Yos, which start as a hobby and end as a habit.

An amazing coincidence and nothing but. In fact the copy-writer had taken the name from an amusing episode in a book by the American author Mark Twain. But Blennerhassett convinced himself the advert was based on him. Throgmorton Street. Pimm's. It all added up.

Completely unable to work that afternoon, he repaired to the sanctuary of his club but was horrified that there too he was met with much mirth. There and then he resolved to sue for libel.

Blennerhassett v. Novelty Sales Services Ltd and Another was heard at the Royal Courts of Justice in the Strand on Thursday, 19 May 1933. But his day at the High Court descended into high farce as Blennerhassett succeeded unintentionally in doing what Groucho Marx, as the attorney Waldorf T. Flywheel of Flywheel, Shyster and Flywheel in a classic radio show, did so brilliantly. The law became a vehicle for humour and Blennerhassett brought the house down.

His counsel stated that 'the advertisement was understood by various persons to refer to him and that it depicted him in a ridiculous and ignominious manner.' He was, stated J.F. Eales KC, 'the only man of that name associated with the Stock Exchange, and in Throgmorton Street, and had for some years eaten at Pimm's Restaurant'.

But as soon as Blennerhassett was cross-examined by the defence lawyer Sir Patrick Hastings the fun started. Witness the transcript highlights.

HASTINGS: The name Blennerhassett is a very well-known Irish name, is it not?

BLENNERHASSETT: Certainly not, it's English.
 (laughter)
HASTINGS: Oh, I didn't mean to cast aspersions on it.
 (laughter) [First point to Hastings.]
HASTINGS: Were you in the habit of eating lobster at
 Pimm's?
BLENNERHASSETT: Much to my cost, I'm afraid I was.
 (laughter)
HASTINGS: And are you a regular there for luncheon?
BLENNERHASSETT: Yes.
HASTINGS: When was the last time you ate there?
BLENNERHASSETT: 1928. (laughter)
HASTINGS: Have you ever played golf at Walton Heath?
BLENNERHASSETT: No.
HASTINGS: Have you ever holed a putt anywhere?
BLENNERHASSETT: No, I don't play golf. (laughter)
HASTINGS: What age do you think the two children are
 in the picture?
BLENNERHASSETT: About five or six.
HASTINGS: Do you have two children?
BLENNERHASSETT: No, one, a son.
HASTINGS: And how old is he?
BLENNERHASSETT: 21. (laughter)
HASTINGS: Tell me, have you any sense of humour?
BLENNERHASSETT: You must ask other people about
 that. (laughter)

After several more exchanges in which Blennerhassett
unfailingly emerged as the fall guy, a stockbroker colleague,
Mr Stubbs, was called as a witness, but succeeded only in
scoring an own goal of head-clutching proportions.

STUBBS: I think the advert does refer to him but also
 people may think he has done it himself to advertise his
 name to the public as a stockbroker, which is against

the Stock Exchange rules. Therefore it is a defamatory innuendo.

HASTINGS: If you wanted to advertise yourself as a member of the Stock Exchange would you select a picture of yourself being escorted into a madhouse with a Yo-Yo? I don't think I should! (gales of laughter)

With each passing exchange Hastings belittled Blennerhassett with consummate skill and not a little poker-faced glee, until the presiding judge, Mr Justice Branson, stepped in to put Blennerhassett out of his misery by stopping the case forthwith: 'No reasonable being would after reading the advertisement have thought it referred to a living person. Even if they did, it is not capable of bearing a defamatory meaning and there is no case to go to the jury.'

Judgment was duly entered for Novelty Sales Services with costs and, next day, *The Times* ran verbatim details of the case across two columns. The entire floor of the Stock Exchange enjoyed their morning read immensely that day, and at Mr Blennerhassett's club the newspapers appeared unusually well thumbed.

William Blennerhassett had succeeded where the advert had failed. His sense-of-humour bypass cost him dear. He had shot himself in the foot. Now he really *did* look ridiculous.

If only he had heeded the wise words of Samuel Johnson (1709–84) on the nature of damage ensuing from libel: 'Very few attacks either of ridicule or invective make much noise but with the help of those they provoke.'

DEATH OF A
SWEET OLD LADY
NEW SOUTH WALES, AUSTRALIA, 1944

On 10 April 1944 at a hospital in Strathfield, near Maitland, New South Wales, the death of 100-year-old Ruth Emilie Kaye aroused no suspicion, and rightfully so.

Miss Kaye was just a sweet old lady. Those who had known her since she arrived in Australia from England more than 50 years before remembered her first as a nurse who had helped lepers and underprivileged girls and later as the caring and well-educated matron of her own nursing home. Make no mistake, Ruth Emilie Kaye was a lady of the right sort.

But what none of her fellow hospital patients knew in 1944 was that the lady they knew as 'Miss Kaye' had been christened Constance Kent 100 years earlier and could have told a tale that would surely have exposed her elderly colleagues to the risk of instant heart failure, a story of one of the most sensational murder trials of Victorian England, which involved an equally sensational mode of confession and is still debated by criminologists to this day. Time travel may not be possible but Ruth Emilie Kaye was proof that if you live long enough, or change your name, the past can indeed become 'another country'.

This is that sweet old lady's story.

Constance Kent was born on 6 February 1844 in Sidmouth, Devon, the ninth child of respectable factory inspector Samuel Kent and his first wife, Mary Anne Windus.

When Mary Anne died in 1853, Samuel Kent married the children's governess, Miss Pratt, and the family moved to Road Hill House at Road (now Rode) on the Somerset-Wiltshire border.

Nine-year-old Constance took the marriage badly. She became moody and unsettled, and when the new Mrs Kent gave birth to a daughter of her own and then a son, Saville, Constance convinced herself that the new members of the family, especially baby Saville, were favoured by their mother.

The night of horror occurred on 29 June 1860, when Constance was 16. In the small hours her stepbrother Saville, aged only three years and ten months, went missing from his cot and was found next morning halfway down the cesspit of a remote old privy in the house's beautiful gardens. His throat had been slashed with a razor and there was a 4-in (10-cm) deep wound in his chest.

The police found many clues and much circumstantial evidence that pointed to Constance as the killer of the innocent child as he slept. Scotland Yard was brought in because of the public outrage at the crime and Inspector Whicher of the Yard became convinced that Constance was guilty, a confused, affection-starved adolescent who had killed in a fit of misguided jealousy.

She was arrested and charged on 20 July 1860 but, at the committal hearing at Devizes on 27 July, Constance's denials were convincing, and Saville's nurse, Elizabeth Gough, gave evidence that the girl's attitude towards her stepbrother had been nothing but a loving one. Although others voiced their suspicions forcibly, there wasn't enough hard evidence to make the accusations stick. Suspicion fell, too, on both Elizabeth Gough and Mr Kent before the case collapsed unsolved, much to Inspector Whicher's chagrin, amid fierce public criticism of 'police incompetence'.

Following Constance's release through lack of evidence, her father sent her away to a convent school in France to help her forget the trauma and she stayed there two years and was noted for her kindness to children. When she returned to England in 1863 she attended a religious retreat, St Mary's Home in Brighton, under the care of the Reverend Arthur Douglas Wagner.

She became convinced there of the value of confession and early in 1865 made a full admission of guilt to Wagner and told him at Easter that she would like to go public.

On 25 April 1865 she went up to London, dressed all in black, walked into the famous Bow Street Magistrates' Court and handed in a written statement. Two days later it was printed in full in *The Times* amid much sensation.

Although there were anomalies in the confession, Constance pleaded guilty to murdering the infant Saville and was duly found so at Wiltshire Assizes in Salisbury on 21 July 1865. The 20-year-old was sentenced to hang and one contemporary reporter wrote that 'her quiet fortitude was such that observers, the jury and even the judge himself could not restrain their tears when he passed sentence, and as he did so, she too pushed back her veil and sobbed uncontrollably'.

With emotions running high, the sentence was commuted to life imprisonment four days later and Constance spent the next 20 years in Millbank, London, and Portland, Dorset, before being released in 1885, aged 41. She maintained throughout that she had committed the crime alone, not from jealousy of Saville, but to avenge her own mother, who she felt had been let down by her father and usurped by his second wife.

Many anomalies remained and many outlandish further theories have been put forward over the years, not least that Constance Kent later became 'Jill', not 'Jack', 'the Ripper'.

That one we *will* discount, but only Constance Kent, Ruth Emilie Kaye to her Australian friends, knew the whole truth of what happened on a summer evening in Rode in 1860 – and she, you will recall, died just a sweet old lady, aged 100, in a New South Wales hospital in 1944.

A DOSE OF ILL FORTUNE

SOUTHPORT, 1947

The air in Southport can be quite bracing but evidently didn't suit the wealthy heiress Amy Victoria Burnett Clements, who died at the Astley Nursing Home there on 27 May 1947.

The death of his wife must have been a particular blow for Dr Robert George Clements because, despite his eminent position in the medical profession, he'd had the incredible misfortune to lose his three previous wives in similar circumstances. In 1912 he had married Edyth Annie Mercier, who tragically expired in 1920. Only the fact that she was a wealthy woman might have softened the crushing blow for Dr Clements.

Newly enriched, he overcame the heartbreak to marry Mary McLeery a year later, but she too expired after just four years of married life. Again, only a substantial inheritance made such tragic misfortune bearable to the unfortunate doctor.

Once more, he mustered the courage to remarry, but Katherine Burke, Mrs Clements number three, died in 1939 of cancer. Although the police became suspicious of such an unlikely hat-trick they didn't conduct an autopsy – such was Dr Clements's grief that he'd had her cremated quickly before it could be carried out.

Remarkably, having suffered more misfortune in 27 years of married life than any man could be expected to endure, he held himself together and met Amy Victoria Burnett. He and 'Vee' got on quite well and when her father died unexpectedly in 1940 the good doctor must have felt she needed the stability that only marriage could offer her. The £22,000 she'd been left was all very well, but what she really needed was a husband. She duly became Mrs Clements number four.

When she had the seizure and went into a coma on 26 May 1947 Dr Clements acted quickly to get her into the nursing home, but she died the next day. He carried out his own diagnosis of myeloid leukaemia and suggested this strongly to his young colleague Dr James Houston, who studied the post-mortem report and duly signed the death certificate despite harbouring personal doubts as to the real cause. Hadn't the staff surgeon, Andrew Brown, noticed the pinpoint pupils of the corpse, sure sign of morphine poisoning? But Dr Houston passed it over.

Grief-stricken once more, Dr Clements quickly arranged the funeral, but this time so many tongues were wagging in Southport that the police stepped in to stop it and ordered a second post-mortem. This concluded that poisoning was indeed the cause of death.

It seemed a certainty that Clements would be charged, found guilty and hanged and that the deaths of all four of his wives would be laid at his door.

Yet Robert George Clements, 57-year-old member of the Royal College of Surgeons, never did stand trial for murder. When police called at his Southport home to arrest him they found his body. He had died from a huge overdose of cyanide administered by his own hand.

Evidently, with five deaths now his responsibility, Clements didn't believe that doctors should save lives. And it was soon to be one more as this extraordinary affair came to its end. On 2 June 1947 Dr Houston, unable to live with the knowledge that he had been professionally negligent, was found dead in his lab. He left his colleagues no room for error at his post-mortem – his body contained 300 times the lethal dose of sodium cyanide.

Dr Robert George Clements joined a small but notorious band of medical men who took life instead of saving it. Indeed for some time he had a reasonable claim to be the doctor with the worst bedside manner of all time, but even as he took his deadly dose in 1947, a sweet little toddler by the name of Harold Frederick Shipman was contemplating his own future as the undisputed holder of that particular title.

CAPSTICK MAKES AN IMPRESSION

BLACKBURN, 1948

Crime detection twenty-first-century style is certainly different from the 1948 variety. DNA profiling and instantaneous computer matching of fingerprints were still in the realms of science fiction back then.

Nor had the police force then established a corporate image. Undying pledges of service and letters to victims headed 'We Care' were simply unheard of. We know we're in safe hands now, but there was nothing so positive in 1948. All the police had then was a sense of duty, due diligence, old-fashioned determination and sensible shoes. Without a 'mission statement' from the constabulary there was surely little hope.

Consider the task facing Detective Chief Inspector John Capstick in May 1948. During the early hours of 15 May three-year-old June Anne Devaney was found to be missing from the ground-floor children's ward of the Queen's Park Hospital in Blackburn, Lancashire. Two-and-a-half hours later she was found in the grounds just 100 yards (91m) away. She had been raped, then brutally murdered, her head having been bashed against a boundary wall.

There were no witnesses to the abduction or murder and all the Blackburn police had to go on were some fingerprints left on a bottle in the ward and a few fibres found on the dead girl's body.

Such was the emotive nature of the crime that the Chief

Constable of Blackburn feared serious public disorder in the town if the crime remained unsolved. He immediately called on Scotland Yard for assistance.

Within a few hours John Capstick and his colleague, Detective Sergeant John Stoneman, arrived from London to take charge. But hopes of an early arrest were dashed when the fingerprints were found not to match those of any known criminal.

The way forward for Capstick was clear as mud. All he had in mind was that the man was likely to be local as he seemed to have knowledge of the hospital layout. But Capstick was made of stern stuff, as his next proposal illustrates.

His suggestion was logical but a touch outrageous. Every male in Blackburn aged between 14 and 90 would be fingerprinted. Only the bedridden would be spared.

The Mayor of Blackburn made a public announcement asking for cooperation and promising that all prints would be destroyed after they had been manually compared with those left by June Devaney's murderer. The phrases 'added to our data bank', 'civil liberties' and 'invasion of privacy' were conspicuously absent as the operation began in earnest.

The first 5,000 prints yielded no match. Nor did the second and third. After 20,000 tries the task looked hopeless. At 30,000 the officers engaged on checking must have been flagging, but no claims for repetitive-strain injury were lodged. The 40,000 mark was duly passed, but on the afternoon of 12 August the cry was 'Eureka!' as set 46,253 yielded a precise match.

That evening 22-year-old Peter Griffiths, a former Guardsman working as a packer in a flour mill, was arrested at his home. No armies of lawyers mobilised in his favour. No social-services personnel rushed to proffer extenuating circumstances on his behalf. Instead, thoroughly ashamed by his actions, Griffiths calmly admitted the offence. His only mitigation was that he had been drunk at the time.

He told the officers who arrested him, 'I hope I get what I deserve,' but pleaded not guilty on the grounds that he had not been responsible for his actions.

Fibres from his suit were quickly matched to those on the body and at the trial at Lancashire Assizes the jury took only 23 minutes to find Peter Griffiths guilty. He was hanged at Walton Prison on 19 November 1948.

It had taken Detective Chief Inspector Capstick three months to bring the killer to justice. Compared with today's techniques his unsophisticated methods were as PC Plod's to the Rapid Response Unit's. It might have been Toytown. And the mayor, no doubt, had worn his ermine-trimmed robes and ceremonial chain when making his impassioned appeal to the doughty burghers of Blackburn from the town hall steps.

But then all life was surreal in 1948. As Griffiths was being held in custody, Manchester United lost 2–1 at home to Derby County, beer was sold at elevenpence (4½p) a pint and 'Big Brother' was the snotty-nosed kid who nicked your gob-stoppers.

Who would ever wish to return to those strange Dark Ages when the police had nothing better to do with their time than catch criminals?

A SUSPENDED SUSPENDED SENTENCE

THE OLD BAILEY, LONDON, 1948

Prior to the abolition of hanging in 1965 the only 'suspended sentence' likely to be accorded to a cold-blooded murderer was the sort that involved a noose around the neck.

Sentence was sometimes mercifully commuted to life imprisonment, it is true, but any bookmaker would have set the odds for Donald George Thomas getting lucky at several thousand to one, for in 1948 Thomas committed the most socially unacceptable crime of that era, murder of a policeman.

In January 1948 a sudden spate of housebreaking and burglary in the Highgate and Southgate areas of north London led police to deploy plain-clothed officers in the locality to keep watch for suspects.

The operation worked. On the evening of 13 February 1948 PC Nathaniel Edgar and his colleague spotted a man behaving suspiciously. When the suspect gave the officers the slip they separated to search the Oaklands Estate in Wynchgate, and at 8.15p.m. several people reported hearing three shots. PC Edgar was found seriously injured and died in the North Middlesex Hospital two hours later. The final entry in his notebook was the name and address of Donald George Thomas, who police records showed had deserted from the army towards the end of the war.

Thomas was on the run from military police for two years before being captured, but again went missing on his release from 160 days' probation. Police quickly formed the opinion that 23-year-old Thomas was their likely murderer and he was traced to lodgings in Mayflower Road, Clapham, where he had holed up with his lover, mother of three Mrs Winkless.

A party of four policemen paid Thomas a surprise early-morning visit, co-opting his landlady Mrs Smeed into the covert ambush operation. Mrs Smeed was to take the couple's breakfast up to their room, leave it outside their door and knock. She performed the role to perfection, only slightly miffed that her culinary magic with the frying pan went entirely to waste.

When Thomas opened his door wearing just his underpants he was greeted by rather more than freshly cooked bacon and eggs and a nice pot of tea, being unceremoniously jumped on by the avenging police presence.

Although Thomas went for the Luger pistol hidden under his pillow, he was overpowered before telling the officers, 'You were lucky. I might just as well be hung for a sheep as a lamb.'

Seventeen rounds of ammunition, a jemmy and a rubber cosh were found in the bedroom and Mrs Winkless, still in bed at the time of the raid, told police that Thomas had confessed to her that he had committed the murder. Thomas unconvincingly denied this and pleaded not guilty.

He was brought to trial at the Old Bailey in April. A police murderer who had loudly voiced further intent, and an army deserter to boot, his cause was as grim as any could be. To nobody's surprise Thomas was found guilty of the murder of PC Edgar and sentenced to death.

Yet to everybody's surprise he lived to tell the tale and was released from prison 14 years later in April 1962, for Thomas had unwittingly selected the only window of opportunity in which to commit his capital crime and remain alive into the bargain – at the time of his conviction the future of capital punishment was being debated in the House of Commons and a temporary suspension of hanging had been enacted during the discussions.

Donald George Thomas's claim to be the luckiest murderer of the twentieth century would seem a valid one, and such was the publicity surrounding the case that it inspired the plot of the 1949 film *The Blue Lamp*, in which the legendary PC George Dixon, of Dock Green fame, played by Jack Warner, was shot and killed by a delinquent played by Dirk Bogarde.

Despite his death halfway through his film debut, Dixon of Dock Green went on to serve many years in the force, single-handedly coining the much-lampooned phrase, 'Evening, all', which has dogged the force ever since.

Nor was the memory of PC Edgar allowed to die, for in 1998 a commemorative fiftieth-anniversary plaque was placed in his honour at Muswell Hill Police Station.

No such affectionate tributes were given to Donald George Thomas, the only police murderer for whom 'suspension' meant life instead of death.

LET'S HEAR IT FOR PARLIAMENT

THE HOUSE OF LORDS, LONDON, 1960

It is easy to forget that the law has to be 'made' by Parliament; tempting, too, to regard the laborious process of British government that steers laws through the upper and lower Houses as being dry, boring and utterly remote from the person in the street.

As a four-year-old child in 1960, I viewed the law as simply the local bobby telling me to be careful as I crossed the road behind the ice-cream van, clutching my cornet for dear life. But little did I know that, as I licked off the last drop of raspberry sauce on a glorious summer's day in 1960, the highest authorities in the land were at that same moment ensconced within the stifling confines of the House of Lords protecting my welfare on that very issue, for Monday, 18 July 1960 was the day of the great ice-cream debate.

I am obliged to *The Times* for revealing verbatim how our great nation's lawmakers go about their business.

PEERS' RESISTANCE MELTS, said the headline to the 'Parliament' column:

The Lord Chancellor took his seat on the woolsack at half past two o'clock to consider the Noise Abatement Bill at Report stage with particular reference to clause 2 regarding the restriction of operation of loudspeakers on highways.

Boring stuff? Not a bit of it, for the fun started as soon as Lord Taylor moved an amendment to permit the use of a speaker between noon and 7p.m. if it was on a vehicle used for the conveyance of a perishable commodity for human consumption (to wit ice-cream) and if it was operated solely for the purposes of informing the public (to wit four-year-old me) that the commodity was for sale and gave no cause for annoyance.

It seems that the drafters of the Bill had entirely ignored the nation's ice-cream men and their peculiarly British chimes and charms, and Lord Taylor, perhaps because he was partial to a choc ice, sought to protect their interests.

Why should the nation's Mr Whippys, Mister Softees and Tonibels be left out in the cold? That was the question for Parliament to debate – and what a lively affair it was.

Lord Taylor met with immediate objections:

LORD REA: I oppose the amendment, not because I don't like ice-cream vendors or their product but because we must remember this is a Noise Abatement Bill, not an Ice-cream Bill. The picture of the Pied Piper of ice-cream men with all the little children following may be appealing but it is false. There has been much lobbying by those interested in the money to be made from ice-cream. That is the truth of it.

LORD TAYLOR: Do you have any evidence?

LORD REA: No, but there is hearsay. It is a rich industry and it would be in their interests for this amendment to pass through.

LORD TAYLOR: That is a monstrous statement. Accusations against an industry should never be hearsay.

As the volume of debate over the Noise Abatement Bill rose ever higher, other Lords of the Realm pitched in:

LORD ATLEE: I concur with Lord Rea. Many people seem to think these chimes an extraordinarily bad nuisance. I have received a pitiful letter from a night watchman whose only time for rest coincides with the very times the bells would be allowed to ring.

LORD AMWELL: I fear we are making ourselves a little ridiculous over the idea of special legislation to deal with a little industry peddling ice-cream up and down the streets. Why not let it be? There are far more infernal noises. Why, every night beneath my window I have motorcycles starting up after midnight. It is abominable. Noise should be dealt with in a fundamental way.

He didn't actually add 'especially when it's underneath my window' but his sorry tale elicited the sympathy of the Minister of Agriculture, who stuck his own two penn'orth in forthwith and provoked gales of laughter from the benches.

LORD WALDEGRAVE: I agree. I hope the House sees fit to allow the amendment. After all, the amendment mentions perishable goods and I read in *The Times* only this morning that vintage port may be considered such a commodity. If we send the Bill back to the Commons unchanged we may lose it altogether and then there would be no control. Surely half a loaf is better than none.

All this talk of food must have aroused another eminent Lord who further unbalanced the menu by introducing a fish course:

LORD MILVERTON: Lord Taylor's speech is a wonderful example of how ice-cream can turn into a red herring. I have a shoal of correspondence commending the house for their help on this issue. I'm not saying the ice-cream lobby are getting at me but privately there has been pressure brought to bear.

I would like to report that someone then shouted 'Stick a flake in it!' Regrettably not, but the response was indignant all the same.

LORD SHACKLETON: I resent the suggestion that the amendment is the result of the ice-cream lobby. No one has approached me!

That sounded suspiciously like a complaint.
LORD BURDEN: Nor me. I know nothing of any ice-cream lobby.

He then rather spoilt the impression of his affected innocence by showing a remarkable insight into the business of Cornish-wafer shifting by adding: 'Without audible means of advertising, the van's sales fall off by 50 to 70 per cent I believe. They perform a useful community service. Are we to prevent small traders earning an honest living?'
LORD SILKIN: The amendment has nothing to do with small traders. It's the big merchants who are behind it.

The continued debate proved all too much for Lord Taylor, who rather felt his fellow peers had lost sight of the issue: 'May I remind this house that the amendment is *not* put down in the interests of any ice-cream people, traders *or* merchants – this Bill is solely in the interests of *noise abatement*,' he shouted vociferously.

It did the trick and with that the amendment was duly agreed. REPRIEVE FOR ICE-CREAM CHIMES, screamed *The Times*'s sub-headline. It was entirely thanks to their Lordships that the children of the sixties were able to contemplate the delights of a 99 and suck on their Zooms and Rockets safe from the fear of the nasty men from the Noise Abatement Office.

So now you know how laws are made and what serious debate goes on in the House of Lords on a typically rigorous day.

TRIAL OF A LADY
THE OLD BAILEY, LONDON, 1960

The year 1960 threw up a number of curious literary cases, but the one heard loud and clear above the rest was the rather dull-sounding *The Crown v. Penguin Books*.

But dull it wasn't, for the case popularly known as the trial of *Lady Chatterley's Lover* caused an entire nation to hold its breath before releasing a gasp of unrepressed relief as the verdict cast aside the final remnants of Victorian prudery in favour of a new era of sexual liberalism, one that made it OK not only to read about 'it', but to talk about 'it' and, glory be praised, to actually do 'it' without having to pretend to the outside world that 'it' didn't really exist.

An apparently routine announcement by Penguin Books on 25 August 1960 set the legal machinery in motion – they intended to publish a 'popular' unexpurgated 3s. 6d. (17½p) paperback edition of D.H. Lawrence's 1928 classic, *Lady Chatterley's Lover*, a book previously available in Britain since 1932 only in an expensive, abridged and much-censored version.

But only a matter of weeks before the proposed publication date, with 200,000 copies already printed awaiting release, the office of the Director of Public Prosecutions informed Penguin that, having read the book, they intended to prosecute under the Obscene Publications Act 1959. The book was put on hold. Not even the best publicity guru could have hyped it better.

The case opened in Court No. 1 at the Old Bailey in London on 20 October 1960; Mr Justice Byrne was the judge, Mervyn Griffith-Jones led the Crown's prosecution, Gerald Gardiner QC fronted the defence, the jury contemplated the huge moral responsibility that their decision would carry and the person in the street contemplated the prospect of reading all the juicy bits if Penguin won – especially pages 176–185.

The prosecution's case was that the book's content would tend to 'deprave and corrupt' those exposed to it. The sex act, they were at pains to point out, was openly described on a number of occasions and the coarseness and vulgarity of both the thought and language that the book contained was 'obscene'. Mervyn Griffith-Jones told the court in the gravest tones possible that he had counted 76 'four-letter words' and he even forced himself to read a selection of them out. The case to him was crystal clear – Lady Constance Chatterley was a shameless adulteress and Mellors, the gamekeeper whose rugged attentions she enjoyed, was nothing but a rough, depraved, sex-crazed degenerate.

The case for the defence encouraged the jury to take a more balanced and modern view. Gerald Gardiner QC said Lawrence's use of four-letter words in the work was merely 'an attempt to talk about sex without shame' and he suggested that all the jury must read the book themselves before passing judgment. As a result of this request, Justice Byrne ordered that a suitable reading room with comfortable armchairs be set up at the Old Bailey and he declared a three-day break for the novel to be read from cover to cover.

Such an unusual interlude created massive public awareness and the newspapers of the day whipped up a frenzy of interest in the affair of 'Lady C'. Certainly public opinion seemed to be moving in favour of the publishers by the time the defence started calling their 35 witnesses on 27 October. A stream of distinguished academics, critics, literary editors, authors and journalists all spoke strongly in favour of the book, and even the Bishop of Woolwich, referring to the 'purple passages' in the prose, suggested that Lawrence was merely 'trying to portray this relationship as an act of holy communion'.

In ending the case for the defence, Gerald Gardiner ridiculed the reactionary views of the prosecution and Mervyn Griffith-Jones did little to dispel the view that he was well out of touch with developments in society when he implored the jury of ordinary men and women to consider 'if the book is one you would even wish your servants to read'.

With that one ludicrous question the case for the prosecution almost certainly foundered. Judge Byrne, though, completed his summing up on day six of the trial in a style that suggested he assumed the jury were repelled by what they had read. He vehemently disparaged the views of the expert witnesses, roundly condemned Lady Chatterley again as a shameless adulteress and implied to the jury that he expected them to 'pass moral judgment on the behaviour the novel describes'.

It took the jury three hours on 2 November 1960 to decide to ignore the judge completely. They had enjoyed the book. 'It' was not a problem. The verdict on 'Lady C' was not guilty.

There was loud clapping and applause from the back of the court and that day's *London Evening Standard* ran a banner headline on its front page, THE INNOCENCE OF LADY CHATTERLEY ... SHE'S CLEARED AFTER 6-DAY TRIAL.

The days that followed witnessed what is surely the most intense physical reaction to any trial decision as queues, mostly of men, formed at the bookshops and street stalls, which announced 'LADY C' NOW ON SALE.

A television reporter famously interviewed some of those making the purchase and astonishingly some men covered their faces with their newspapers or issued a terse 'no comment' when asked why they were buying the book.

One rather prim-looking woman, meanwhile, asserted very firmly, 'I'm buying it for someone else.'

Needless to say, despite this rather furtive reaction from some quarters, the book became a bestseller. Judge Byrne, meanwhile, severely piqued at the jury's decision, never presided at another trial as the shameless 'Lady C' led a newly liberated Britain into the 'Swinging Sixties'.

A VERY QUIET TENANT

RHYL, NORTH WALES, 1960

At first glance the Quarterly Assizes records for Ruthin, Denbighshire, for 1960 wouldn't suggest anything unusual about the trial of 65-year-old widow Mrs Sarah Harvey.

Falsely obtaining £2 a week under a court order that had in truth become invalid some time ago was naughty but hardly sensational. But it was certainly macabre that she had claimed it on behalf of a woman who had been dead fully 20 years. And that the claims had persisted throughout that time smacked of deliberate deception rather than absent-mindedness. Maybe it was fair after all that the seemingly harmless pensioner got 15 months in prison.

Yet the bare facts hide a much stranger story. Had it been a classic Hammer Horror film it might well have been considered too far-fetched to be believable. This is the tale of Sarah Harvey and her lodger Mrs Frances Knight, the quietest tenant of all time.

It was early in 1939 that semi-invalid Frances Knight moved into the home of Sarah Harvey. She was around for only a matter of months, apparently just passing through.

It was 21 years later, when Mrs Harvey was away for a few days in hospital, that her taxi-driver son Leslie decided to surprise his mother by redecorating the house. But Les got the surprise of *his* life when curiosity got the better of him and he forced open the door of the landing cupboard with a screwdriver – he remembered from childhood it was always locked. Now was his chance, on 5 May 1960, to reveal its secret.

There dressed in bedraggled nightdress and dressing gown was a cobweb-covered mummified body. Never a nice discovery – but especially chilling in the very year that Alfred Hitchcock's *Psycho* was showing at the cinema. The dry hair and hollow gaze had a definite whiff of Norman Bates's mother.

Les called the police and when their surgeon arrived he found the corpse rigid and stuck to the linoleum floor – using a garden spade to prise it loose he concluded the mummification was due to the circulation of air via a gap in the door frame. The dead woman might have had an illness but at least she'd been 'cured' in a manner of speaking.

Forensic examination suggested the body was that of a female aged between 50 and 60 with a pronounced limp. When Mrs Harvey was interviewed she confirmed it was her lodger Mrs Knight. She said she had found her dead after a bout of illness just months after she moved in. Unsure what to do she had hidden the body in the cupboard.

The police accepted the body was Frances Knight but were suspicious of marks on the neck indicating possible strangulation with a stocking. Sarah Harvey was charged with murder.

During the five-day trial she strenuously denied it. And experts suggested death was due to disseminated sclerosis, from which Mrs Knight was known to have suffered. The jury found Sarah Harvey innocent of murder but guilty of claiming Mrs Knight's £2 a week.

Did she kill her lodger? Only Mrs Harvey knew, but what is certain is that Frances Knight was the only tenant in history to pay £2 a week to live in a cupboard for 21 years without once complaining to her landlady.

A MOVING EXPERIENCE
THE HIGH COURT, LONDON, 1970

There is an apparently trifling geographical distinction between London's two most famous court buildings. The Royal Courts of Justice, sometimes referred to as the High Court or more commonly simply the Law Courts, are in the Strand. The Central Criminal Court, meanwhile, generally known as the Old Bailey, is merely a stroll down Fleet Street away, less than a mile (1.6km) distant.

But that puts only the Old Bailey in the City of London itself, and it was this fact that proved significant enough one day in 1970 for general mayhem to ensue.

There are some who say that there is no such thing as a truly effective short cut, but when the case load at the Old Bailey began to outstrip the court's capacity it seemed a pretty good idea to transfer some of the backlog to the Royal Courts of Justice.

One such case concerned a matter of fraudulent dealing by the directors of the crashed 'Rolls Razor' Washing Machine Company and the expected marathon trial began on Wednesday, 8 April. But, only seconds after Mr Justice MacKenna took to his seat in New Court No. 4 to commence proceedings, there was an unexpected turn of events.

A juror asked to be excused duty because his wife was ill, and was immediately granted that privilege. This was by no means unusual – a new juror would be quickly commandeered and sworn in without delay. Or so the judge thought.

Not so, My Lord. A barrister was quick to point out that under the Supreme Court of Judicature Act of 1873 jurors in cases originally allocated to courts within the City could be sworn in only in the City itself. He might have been a jobsworth but he was darn well right and months of tortuous proceedings could have been made invalid at a stroke on such a technicality.

There was only one thing for it. In order to conduct the swearing-in procedure properly and kick off the case in a valid manner the entire court needed to decamp temporarily to the Old Bailey.

It was at this point that the vagaries of legal hierarchy emerged to graphic effect, for the judge travelled in his official chauffeur-driven car, the barristers hailed taxis and the jurors were allotted Shanks's Pony.

After the valiant eleven's unscheduled walk they met the somewhat bemused twelfth man at the Old Bailey and he was duly sworn in within the City confines 57 minutes after the adjournment.

Then it was back to the High Court, the judge by chauffeur-driven private car, the barristers by taxi and the full complement of jurors again on foot. That the smooth operation of the machinery of British justice should have been disturbed by such a spanner in the works was certainly embarrassing at the start of such a high-profile trial but there was more to come.

Back in Court No. 4 the number of jurors still didn't add up and there was a near panic when an usher was heard to say, dispensing with any pretence to legal jargon, 'Blimey, only nine of 'em have come back.' Much to the judge's relief the missing three were quickly rounded up – they had got lost after a visit to the court toilets – and the case commenced at 12.10p.m., nearly two hours after it should have started.

Embarrassing, yes, but just one of those excusable one-offs that will happen. Well, two-offs actually, for as Court No. 4 settled down to normality there was a stir in the adjacent Court No. 5 as Judge Grant was about to begin a long and complicated income tax case.

A woman juror, it appeared, feared her delicate health would not stand the strain of a lengthy trial. Again, a twelfth person was needed. Again the procession began – first the limo, then the taxis and finally the footsloggers. As they scurried along to the Old Bailey as if their lives depended on it, passing tourists must have thought they were witnessing a quaint Olde English custom, the ancient art of court racing, perhaps. In any case, they made it back to Court No. 5 in record time, bang on schedule for the lunch adjournment.

Wednesday, 8 April 1970, wasn't the proudest day in English legal history but it was the only day two judges, a score of barristers and 24 jurors went court-hopping at the behest of a barrister whose anorak knowledge of an 1873 Act led to this strangely moving experience.

CAREERS ADVICE
YORK CROWN COURT, 1971

Burglary may not appear in the careers books but that hasn't stopped thousands of young hopefuls joining the ranks since time immemorial to see if they can make it pay.

Much to the cost of their victims, there are some burglars who have done 'very well, thank you' from this unusual job, but it is heartening to know that there have also been spectacular failures. And they don't come more spectacular than Philip McCutcheon.

Having been arrested for the twentieth time, on this occasion after driving his getaway car into two parked vans, Mr McCutcheon appeared at York Crown Court in 1971. It was an appearance that might have touched even the most hard-hearted of the anti-burglar lobby, for McCutcheon, it has to be said, just didn't look the part.

The judge was certainly affected for, in giving McCutcheon a conditional discharge, Recorder Rodney Percy gave what must be the most heartfelt and brutally honest advice ever delivered from the bench:

'May I advise that I really think you should give burglary up,' he said. 'You have a withered hand, an artificial leg and only one eye. You have been caught in Otley, Leeds, Harrogate, Norwich, Beverley, Hull and York. How can you hope to succeed? You are a rotten burglar. You are always being caught.' Well said, that man. Sounder careers advice has seldom been given.

It is tempting to suggest that Philip McCutcheon is the worst burglar of all time but in fairness to him, and as this is *The Law's Strangest Cases*, it would be remiss of me not to mention a number of other candidates for the title.

Strong contender from Europe is the Parisian burglar who, on 4 November 1933, attempted to rob the home of an antique dealer. By way of disguise, lest he should be disturbed, he dressed in a fifteenth-century suit of armour. If only he'd stuck to the more traditional black-and-white hooped shirt, mask and bag marked swag (strangely seldom seen these days), he might have fared better, for the clanking of the suit of armour awoke the owner, who pushed the burglar off balance, dropped a small sideboard across his breastplate and called the police.

The burglar was cross-examined while still in his suit, and confessed all: 'Yes, I am a thief,' said a muffled voice through the visor. 'I thought I would frighten the owner in this.'

As if that weren't sufficient embarrassment, there was still more to come. It was 24 hours before the hapless thief could be prised from his badly dented metal suit, during which time he was fed breakfast through the visor.

Could anyone possibly top our Frenchman? Well, if everything really is bigger and better in the USA, that must include cock-ups. Take a bow, Charles A. Meriweather, who in Baltimore in 1978 broke into a house, confronted the woman occupant and demanded money. Although she said she had only loose change, Meriweather's acutely sharp brain was at work in an instant: 'Write me a cheque,' he barked. 'Who shall I make it out to?' asked the woman. 'Charles A. Meriweather,' came the immediate reply.

He was arrested a few hours later.

So that's Britain, Europe and the USA all in the running for the worst burglar of all time. Not wishing to be accused of geographical bias, I'll finish in the East.

In January 1998 a thief pulled off a sensational coup when

he fled from the Yanmonoki Museum in central Japan clutching a 600-year-old Chinese platter dating from the Ming dynasty and worth an estimated £260,000. It was just like a scene from a movie.

A Laurel and Hardy movie, that is, for the thief dropped the platter in the road as he made his escape and saw it shatter into fragments.

Still tempted to think that crime might pay? Then you will probably ignore the sensible careers advice of Rodney Percy and listen instead to that given by Woody Allen in the film *Take the Money and Run* (1969). As the eager criminal Virgil Starkwell, he justifies his job in a classic one-liner: 'I think crime pays. The hours are good. You travel a lot.'

A QUESTION OF ENTRY

COLCHESTER, 1971

Even the dry *All England Law Reports* have their moments.
A senior judge described *The Crown v. Collins* at appeal as
'about as extraordinary a case as I have ever heard. Were the
facts put into a novel or portrayed on the stage they would
be regarded as so improbable as to be unworthy of serious
consideration and as verging on farce.'

Although the case involved a serious question of rape, the
acquittal of Collins on appeal and the nature of the narrative
have rendered it almost a music-hall-joke.

Here is a heady mix of *Romeo and Juliet*, *Confessions of a
Window Cleaner* and the best tradition of Whitehall farce
with enough double entendres and tacky innuendo thrown
in for several remakes of *Carry on Dick*.

Recorded in the manner of 'P.G. Wodehouse meets Jilly
Cooper' it is one of the few cases that legal professionals
remember almost verbatim from their days as law students.

The basic facts are that, on 29 October 1971 at Essex
Assizes, 19-year-old Stephen William George Collins was
convicted of forcibly entering a house in Colchester in the
early hours of 24 July 1971 with intent to rape. He was given
a 21-month prison sentence against which he appealed
and the conviction was subsequently quashed by Edmund
Davies in the Court of Appeal on 5 May 1972.

The All England Law Reports rather quaintly relate that
'one evening the appellant had had a good deal to drink and

was desirous of having sexual intercourse'. The narrative they then regale us with is a very lengthy one but the essence was that Collins, on spotting an open window to a first-floor room, which he knew to be the bedroom of an 18-year-old girl he was acquainted but not intimate with, decided he would chance his luck.

The girl shared the house with her mother, so clandestine entry was paramount. He secured a step-ladder, climbed it and peeped in to see the girl naked and asleep on her bed immediately beneath the window. He descended the ladder again and removed all his clothes with the exception, mindful of preserving the finest tradition of British manhood, of his socks. He later told the court that this was better to facilitate his escape should the girl's mother seek to interrupt the amorous proceedings.

Collins's version of events was that he then ascended the ladder again and before any part of his body crossed the threshold of the open window the girl beckoned him in and then pulled him down on to the bed, where 'full intimate relations' ensued.

The girl's version of events was that after having spent the evening consuming a not inconsiderable amount of alcohol with her boyfriend she had gone to bed and later awoken to see a blond man in a state of 'obvious arousal' looking into her bedroom. She had indeed beckoned him in and undeniably 'willingly engaged in intimacy'. It was only after the event that she realised Collins wasn't the man she believed him to be.

The Law Reports take up the tale:

When she saw the naked male form in the moonlight she jumped to the conclusion that it was her boyfriend, with whom she was on terms of regular and frequent sexual intimacy, coming to pay her an ardent nocturnal visit. It was only after the lapse of some time that the length of his hair and tone of voice suggested to her that there was something 'different' about him, so she switched on the bedside light whereupon she realised it was Collins rather than her boyfriend. She slapped him on the face and then told him to leave, which he did, via the ladder, and the girl strongly asserted that she would never have agreed to full intimacy had she known the man was not her boyfriend.

It's all very tricky, there's no doubt about it, for Collins's claim was that he simply thought he'd 'got lucky'. Among many issues debated at great length at the appeal hearing, the question of 'entry' proved central and the 5-in (12.7-cm) wide threshold of the window became the focus of the whole case. If any part of Collins's body had crossed the threshold 'before' he was beckoned in then his entry was deemed to be uninvited and his intention one of rape. If the beckoning occurred before he had begun to cross the threshold then his entry was deemed to be an invitation and the 'willing act' that followed a legitimate consequence of that invitation.

The debate about whether 'any' part of Collins's body had entered the building 'uninvited' has given rise to much rampant embellishment in subsequent retellings. The 'one glass too many' version has Collins entering the 'wrong' house, believing it to be that of 'his' girlfriend, and the window slamming shut to cut short his ardour in the most eye-watering fashion.

But the sober facts are that the Appeal Court found that Stephen Collins was deemed not to have forced entry. As such his place in the annals of law's strangest cases remains that of an innocent but red-faced Romeo.

A SOUND (ASLEEP) VERDICT

LEWES ASSIZES, 1971

When two young brothers were convicted of murder at Lewes Assizes in November 1971 their future looked undeniably grim, but they were to launch an appeal of unprecedented novelty (for a murder case), which put the validity of their conviction under far closer scrutiny than the trial judge, Mr Justice Crichton, had ever bargained for.

The evidence against Alan and Keith Langham had been particularly strong. It seems they had entered the home of an elderly Hastings resident, Charles Levett, intent on burglary and ended up stabbing him. Twice in the back and 12 times in the chest was the count, and they broke three knives in the frenzy of the vicious murder.

The brothers' defence that the gentleman had made 'indecent advances' towards them was entirely rejected by the jury and Judge Crichton found them both guilty of murder and sentenced them to life.

But the brothers had a solicitor who kept a close eye on cases of the strange variety and he was aware of the unusual facts surrounding the 1961 case of *The Crown v. Edworthy*. On that occasion Ernest Edworthy, a Royal Army Pay Corps officer, had been court-martialled at Ashton-under-Lyne, Lancashire, for fraudulent financial dealings while serving in Sierra Leone, but the decision was overturned at appeal after Edworthy's legal advisers claimed that the judge, Mr Acland-Hood, had been asleep during important passages of the trial. A close scrutiny of the judge's summing up revealed significant omissions and errors and this was taken as sufficient evidence that he had indeed nodded off during proceedings.

The Langham brothers had complained several times to their solicitor during their trial that Judge Crichton 'was asleep' and those complaints resulted in an unusual affidavit from their solicitors, which looked likely, in the light of the Edworthy precedent, to get them off: 'When the evidence was coming to an end and counsel's speeches were beginning,' it read, 'the judge at about 12 noon was sitting with his head resting on his hands, his eyes shut and his head nodding, and for approximately the next 15 minutes he was manifestly asleep from time to time.'

Such a vehement sworn statement presented Lord Widgery and his colleagues with a tricky problem indeed when the case came to the Court of Appeal in April 1972. Were they to be forced by precedent to sanction the unconditional release of two brutal murderers on such an embarrassing technicality? The newspaper headlines just didn't bear thinking about: DOZY JUDGE GIVES MURDERERS' RELEASE THE NOD.

It is not for me to suggest that their Lordships closed ranks, nor would I advocate that the release of the murderers would have been any sort of justice in the real sense, but I have to report that, faced with an undoubted dilemma, they came up with a corker of a decision. After the most detailed scrutiny of Judge Crichton's summing up, their findings were that he had simply been 'thinking with his eyes shut'.

Judge Crichton's summing up, it appeared, included definite reference to evidence given during the period he was accused of being in the land of Nod. That was sufficient for the appeal panel to find that he only 'appeared to be asleep'.

The Langhams' advisers were hugely put out by what they saw as an abject whitewash and they forcibly suggested that even 'appearing' to be asleep was at best exceptionally rude and at worst a 'reverse' contempt of court.

Lord Widgery, the Lord Chief Justice, listened intently to the argument, with his eyes open it should be said, but remained unmoved: 'The judge was not asleep,' he asserted, 'and if he appeared to be, however unfortunate and however much to be deplored that might be, it was not a ground for saying that justice was not seen to be done.'

As a result of that unequivocal statement, and despite a long letter of complaint from the Langham boys' mother, the brothers were detained at Her Majesty's pleasure for some considerable time. Few would disagree that the decision was 'right' in a moral sense but there is an important legal precept to be learnt here. Whenever you see a judge asleep it would be wise not to insult him, take his name in vain or even pull a face because, being all-seeing and not at all like us ordinary mortals, he will merely be 'thinking with his eyes shut'.

WHAT A DIFFERENCE A DAY MAKES

GLASGOW, SCOTLAND, 1972

When Joseph Beltrami started his business as a young lawyer in Glasgow's Buchanan Street in 1958, there was no guarantee he would make a name for himself.

Yet by 1972 he had become Glasgow's leading criminal lawyer and the favourite of that city's notorious underworld. 'If you want to get off, get Joe Beltrami' was the word on the street, for he was known not to miss a trick.

Yet some cases look pretty hopeless from the start. One such arose from an armed robbery early in 1972 at the Stepps Hotel on the Edinburgh Road. Sawn-off shotguns were used and around £2,000 was stolen.

It was a matter of days before James H. Steele and another youth were arrested. Substantial amounts of money were recovered from both men, witnesses made positive identifications, and police claimed to have full confessions. All the prisoners had was a good lawyer. They had 'got Beltrami'.

That was the gloomy scenario facing Joseph Beltrami as he applied unsuccessfully for bail for his new clients. They were duly committed for trial at Glasgow High Court but various delays meant the trial date had to be fixed for some months ahead.

It was a few days before the Monday on which the trial was due to start that Beltrami first saw a chink of light when he mused over the terms of the Criminal Procedure (Scotland)

Act 1887, which limited the time the accused could be held in custody if refused bail. Although the act has now been amended, it stated clearly in 1975 that 'the accused must be brought to trial, and the trial concluded, within 110 days of their initial committal for the offence'.

Beltrami consulted his diary, counted carefully and calculated that the one hundred and tenth day would expire at midnight on the Tuesday, the second day of the scheduled trial. He reasoned that the Crown had just two days to complete a complicated trial involving more than 50 witnesses. He knew they were fully au fait with the 110-day rule but he was sure they would struggle to meet it. Their task had been made even harder by the arrest of a third suspect six weeks after the first two, who, even though well within the time limit himself, was still part of the same trial. It would all take time.

The Crown, however, seemed quite relaxed, and on the first day proceedings were adjourned at 4.30p.m. Apparently there was no rush. Beltrami and his team kept their heads down, not even telling the prisoners that the clock was ticking, so they thought, in their favour.

Tuesday's proceedings began unflurried and again the Crown prosecution team seemed ultra-cool. This time the court adjourned at 4.15p.m. Beltrami went home fully expecting a frantic phone call that night from a Crown representative seeking the formal grant of an extension, but none came.

Only on the way into court on Wednesday did Beltrami hear two of the opposition speaking with some resolve: 'We've got to finish today and we will do, even if we sit until midnight,' they said. By their diaries, it seemed, the one hundred and tenth day was the Wednesday.

Again Beltrami counted meticulously before taking the plunge and ordering his counsel to make a bold statement: 'The first and second accused have now been detained in custody for a greater period than the maximum permitted by law. They are now entitled to be liberated and declared free for all time for the crime with which they are charged.'

Crown prosecution officials looked flustered. Judge Lord Leecham raised a quizzical eyebrow, sent the jury out and took advice. When he called the jury back he explained that 'owing to some mistake I must ask you to return formal verdicts of not guilty on the two men'.

The stunned prisoners were liberated. Even the third accused had cause for celebration when later the same day the court returned on him that peculiarly Scottish 'halfway-house' verdict of 'not proven'.

Beltrami had triumphed against all odds. That the case has since become known as 'the Leap Year Case' is the key to his victory: 1972 was a leap year and two armed robbers had been saved by Beltrami's diligence in including the intervening day 29 February in his calculations.

Not surprisingly a somewhat embarrassed Crown Office ordered an immediate enquiry. The same mistake has never occurred again. The freed prisoners celebrated their strange victory with wild celebrations. What a difference a day made.

AN UNCOMMONLY VIOLENT PROTEST

IPSWICH MAGISTRATES' COURT, 1972

Violence in court isn't common, but occasionally parties feeling sufficiently wronged have sought instant vengeance by non-peaceful means.

Generally the accused goes for the judge. But victims or their relatives sometimes target the accused. More rarely solicitors have engaged in open combat, jurors failing to agree have reached the daggers-drawn stage, and even judges have sought to exercise their powers by more physical means than their jurisdiction allows.

But scarcely is uncourtly behaviour more bizarre than that at Ipswich Magistrates' Court on Thursday, 27 April 1972.

In the dock was 23-year-old Anthony Francis Joseph Judge, charged with two blackmail offences. The sums of £5 and £10 to which the charges related suggest that his 'information' was hardly red-hot, but the magistrates ruled that he had a case to answer and ordered that he should be remanded in custody pending a later trial at Ipswich Crown Court.

Not fancying a spell inside, Judge's immediate thoughts turned to violence. But of a peculiar kind, for his choice of target was a strange one.

With an impassioned cry of 'I do not want to go to prison,' he whipped a razor blade out of his pocket and slashed at his own throat. Death was evidently preferable to life inside. Maybe he'd heard bad reports about the food.

Only the prompt action of his solicitor Alan Barker saved the day as he jumped on his client to wrest the razor blade from him. The life of the accused was duly saved by this heroic defence but both men left court in an ambulance, the prisoner with a slashed neck and his solicitor a badly cut hand.

As acts of vengeance go, the behaviour of Anthony Judge was certainly uncommon. Yet amazingly not one of the newspapers reporting the case saw fit to use the headline of the century: JUDGE SLASHES THROAT IN COURT – now there *was* an opportunity missed.

And finally, while we're on the subject of offensive weapons in court, it would be unforgivable not to mention the Frenchman who caused something of a stir during his divorce hearing in Cologne in 1995. Evidently intent on topping Anthony Judge's razor-blade performance in some spectacular fashion, he was discovered to have a Japanese ceremonial sword, with a 3-ft (0.9-m) blade, concealed in his trouser leg. When he was asked to explain himself, his reasoning was ingenious if not a little improbable.

Not even the German court's knowledge that the French bake bread of an entirely unnecessary length could add credence to the defendant's classic answer: 'It was in case there was a long delay before my case came up. I was planning to use it to make my sandwiches.'

A FRUITLESS WAIT
THE HIGH COURT, LONDON, 1974

Assessing damages for alleged libel or breach of contract can be tricky. The subjective system has produced both triumphant winners and disgruntled losers.

It is not unusual for huge damages to be awarded after a lengthy court case; nor is it uncommon for a derisory award to be made after only a short hearing. Somewhat rarer would be the award of a large cheque after only a brief court case. But the oddity of them all is the award of only nominal damages after a marathon hearing.

And the daddy of that particular field is the 1974 classic of *Evans Marshall & Co. Ltd v. Bertola*.

Evans Marshall, a Regent Street wine merchant, had signed a sole agency distribution agreement with the Spanish sherry producer Bertola. Bertola's sherry was the really good stuff, for they were based in Jerez itself, the town from which the distinctive fortified wine gets its very name. The London wine merchants were justifiably pleased that they alone would be dictating which of Britain's 'just-one-more-small-glass' brigade of maiden aunts would be tippling the precious liquid.

But alas the agreement was broken when Bertola started supplying Evans Marshall's rivals. The wine merchants duly sued for substantial damages and thus began one of the longest commercial law actions ever heard in England. The case reached its climax in the High Court on Thursday,

17 January 1974. Two QCs, six barristers, nearly a dozen solicitors and Judge Justice Ackland had studied both the solid facts and alleged fictions long and hard. They had pored over 31 bundles of associated documents and Judge Ackland's final summation lasted four-and-a-half hours. The total costs of the hearing ran well into six figures.

As Judge Ackland neared the end it became clear he was about to uphold the wine merchants' claim and as he finally reached the important bit involving the pound signs the Evans Marshall hierarchy held their breath.

Only two questions concerned them. What figure would follow the pound sign? And how many noughts would follow that?

The answer to the first was 2; the answer to the second might have been 000,000 or 00,000 or even a disappointing 0,000. In the event it wasn't even 000, or 00 or even 0. In fact there were no zeros whatsoever – Judge Ackland had upheld their claim and awarded them only £2, explaining that 'the "damages" in this case are only nominal because Evans Marshall had not suffered any damage'.

It was a cruel blow, although there is always a risk of being dealt the 'nominal award' card in this gambling area of the law. But what the unsuccessful litigants really found hard to swallow was that it had taken precisely 72 days to reach that conclusion.

This remarkable case set a new record for length-damages ratios in commercial actions: for each day in court Evans Marshall had accrued precisely 2.77 (recurring) pence.

Whether they spent the £2 on a couple of glasses of sherry to drown their sorrows remains unrecorded. If they did, it probably wasn't one of Bertola's – nor did a glass of QC seem entirely appropriate in the circumstances.

THE TRUTH, PARTLY THE TRUTH AND EVERYTHING BUT THE TRUTH

THE HIGH COURT, LONDON, 1975

WOMAN WINS LIBEL ACTION AGAINST SON: *The Times* headline of 17 July 1975 was a genuine rarity. Mother-versus-son court cases are most uncommon.

Yet Mrs Ada Hill of Stourbridge had no reason to be anything but proud of her son Archibald when he first announced that he was writing his autobiography containing many reminiscences of his childhood.

Mrs Hill probably envisaged the sort of idyllic world recounted by Laurie Lee in his 1959 classic *Cider with Rosie*. She looked forward to reading her son's work and might well have mused on the title he would choose – *Days of Sunshine* would be nice, or perhaps something deeper like *The Hills of Plenty; Mother Knew Best* had a nice ring to it, too. She might even cope with *Tizer with Roger*, for these were after all enlightened times.

When *Cage of Shadows* was published by Hutchinson and Co. there might have been a fleeting moment in which Mrs Hill would like to have believed that her dear Archie had written the account through the eyes of his pet budgerigar. But when she read the book and remembered they had never had a budgerigar, she was in for a most unpleasant surprise.

Cage of Shadows was Archibald Hill's account of 'the poverty-ridden years of his childhood' and 'a stirring protest against the abject suffering of the 1930s depression era'. Oh, dear!

Ada was not best pleased. Hadn't she scrimped and scraped to do her best for little Archie all those years ago? Was this the thanks she got for her years of sacrifice? She took the only reasonable course open to a wronged mother – Ada Hill sued.

Hill v. Hutchinson and Co. and Hill was heard at the High Court in London on 16 July 1975 and proved a triumph for Ada. Mr Justice Eveleigh heard that the publishers had already withdrawn the book temporarily and removed the passages that criticised Mrs Hill for the way she brought up young Archie, now aged 48.

The issue of monetary damages was discussed but all Mrs Hill really wanted was a public apology. Archibald was dutifully repentant: 'I now see that my mother was as much a victim of that era as myself,' he announced, 'and some of my allegations based on childhood recollections were misconceived. I apologise to mother unreservedly.'

Unlike *Cider with Rosie*, *Cage of Shadows* hardly took the literary world by storm. But lest anyone should believe that all in the golden-tinged Cotswolds world of Laurie Lee was perpetual sunshine, I'm afraid I have to refocus the image, for *Cider with Rosie* also landed its author in the High Court in the most acrimonious circumstances. The offending passage on page 272 of Lee's world-renowned 'evocation of a Cotswold childhood' seemed harmless enough:

I remember very clearly how it started. It was summer, and we boys were sitting on the bank watching a great cloud of smoke in the sky. A man jumped off his bike and cried, 'It's the piano-works!' and we ran the four miles to see it. There was a fire at the piano-works almost every year, it seemed to be a way of balancing the books.

But Lee's short note in the front of his book proved prophetic: 'The book is a recollection of early boyhood, and some of the facts may be distorted by time.'

Lee on that count was spot-on, for the piano-factory episode was pure fabrication and both the long-established firm in Stroud and their insurance company were much put out by the defamatory (and inflammatory) comments.

That the book was withdrawn within a fortnight of their complaint and that in subsequent editions the piano factory became a 'boiler-factory' was not sufficient for the firm. Lee had struck a wrong note and they wanted a personal apology and damages. On 18 July 1960 *Stroud Piano Company Limited v. Lee* was heard in the High Court and the suitably cowed author was ordered to pay £5,000 compensation.

The postscript to this particular case was that the veracity of *all* Lee's writing subsequently came under scrutiny: 'If we know that one episode in the book is untrue, can we have any confidence in other episodes?' wrote a correspondent in *John O'London's Weekly*, and much of Lee's later writing was dogged by similar doubts.

Laurie Lee didn't suffer too badly from this curious episode and he had a novel theory on the essence of truth that, if it was ever accepted by the courts of law, would change the course of legal history forever:

'Memory can be more real than events,' he wrote in his notebook. And in his essay on 'Writing Autobiography' he asserted: 'In writing autobiography, especially one that looks back at childhood, the only truth is what you remember.'

With that in mind, the time I scored 300 before lunch for England against the Australians at Lord's on my ninth birthday is a story I must write down sometime.

A NOTE OF CAUTION
CROYDON CROWN COURT, 1978

Drugs trials are not renowned for their entertainment value. But one in Croydon on 7 November 1978 had a definite note of interest – the 'wrong note' for a particularly hapless juror.

Although the defence barrister was fighting his client's corner for all he was worth, 69-year-old Judge Jean Hall seemed intent on giving him a particularly hard time from the bench. Being rather 'old school' she exchanged sharp words with him on a number of occasions and this evidently aroused the sympathy of a male member of the jury, who communicated this to the defence barrister by passing him a note.

While it is perfectly in order for the jury to communicate with the judge in such a way, it is irregular for a juror to send notes, on whatever subject, to the defence. Who knows what message they might convey? A threat, a bribe, vital evidence?

It was typical of Judge Hall that she didn't miss a trick and sure enough she spotted the note being passed and duly asked to read it. If the juror seemed a little uneasy it was no surprise, as the note of sympathy asked, 'How would you like that as a mother-in-law?'

Retribution was swift and despite an apology from the juror he was summarily dismissed, one of only a few jurors 'sent off' for their conduct in all legal history.

On the subject of notes and jurors it would be impossible

to let pass the opportunity to retell an incident said to have occurred in a rape trial at a Northern crown court in the late 1970s.

According to the account of the local newspaper reporter, when the young woman victim was asked to repeat, for the benefit of the jury, the words said to her by her attacker prior to the incident she was somewhat embarrassed to do so in open court. She was therefore allowed to write the extremely coarse phrase down for it to be passed along the row of jurors. The sanitised translation of the words she wrote on the note would be something along the lines of 'I'm going to give you the most thorough going over you've ever had.'

It proved significant that the male juror on the end of the row had nodded off during this passage of the trial and he had to be nudged awake by the attractive woman juror next to him as she passed him the folded note, which he read before giving her a wink and hastily pocketing the evidence. When the judge asked for the piece of paper back the juror replied, 'I'd rather not, it's a personal matter.'

The name of the poor chap escapes me but there is little doubt that later that day he duly became the most disappointed juror of all time. Or at least I assume he did.

A PICTURE PAINTS A THOUSAND WORDS
NEW YORK, UNITED STATES, 1980

They say 'a picture paints a thousand words' and a New York jury seemed intent on proving the accuracy of that old chestnut when they delivered a verdict in December 1980 that made US legal history.

Central to their deliberations was the unusual question of whether a person could be libelled by a painting, for a New York artist, Paul Georges, had allegedly been rather more expressive with his brush strokes than two of his arty rivals would have liked.

This being New York, there was only one course of action for Jacob Silberman and Anthony Siani when they saw Georges's *The Mugging of the Muse*: they sued.

The large-scale allegorical work showed three men with knives about to attack a partly nude young woman, the 'muse of art', in a dark alleyway. What incensed the two artists was that the masks on two of the faces were clearly 'theirs' and they subsequently told the court that they were 'being ridiculed not only as violent criminals but as artists intent on murdering art'. Both the supposedly vilified artists had first asked Georges to change the faces so that they could not be recognised, but he refused to compromise: 'The role of an artist is to find a pictorial truth and this is not the same as literary or photographic truth,' he pleaded.

But the jury disagreed, finding Georges guilty of libelling his two rivals, who received $30,000 each in damages. It was a landmark decision in US legal history, which served as a warning to all artists of the future that using 'dirty brushes' might cost them dear, but it was by no means the first legal sparring in the artistic community.

Back in 1877 the Massachusetts-born painter James McNeill Whistler, then living and working in England, sued the distinguished art critic John Ruskin for libel after Ruskin had conducted not so much a smear campaign as a 'splatter' campaign against Whistler's modern Impressionist style. On viewing Whistler's *Nocturne in Black and Gold*, which somewhat vaguely depicted a firework display over the Thames, Ruskin was moved to write, 'I never expected to hear a coxcomb ask two hundred guineas for flinging a pot of paint in the public's face.'

Appearing before Judge Sir John Huddleston at London's Courts of Justice in November 1878, Whistler, who had sued for a massive 1,000 guineas, gave a good account of himself as examples of his art were paraded before the court. Asked by Ruskin's defence counsel, 'Did you really ask two hundred guineas for the work of just two days?', Whistler responded instantly: 'No. It was for the knowledge gained through a lifetime.' Maybe he'd been taking lessons from young Oscar Wilde, master of the clever riposte and in time himself to be a tragic victim of a famously unsuccessful libel action.

At any rate Whistler triumphed in his own action as the jury found that he had indeed been libelled, but his joy was quickly quelled when he heard the amount of damages: a paltry farthing! On top of that indignity the judge pronounced a judgment of 'no costs', so Whistler had to foot his own legal bill for nearly £500. The only compensation was that Ruskin, too, had to find £386 to defray his own expenses.

The report in *The Examiner* got it about right when they described the outcome of the case as 'A victory which bears a very striking resemblance to a defeat'.

A salutary lesson to paint merchants of all eras and styles, perhaps. Whether it's twentieth-century New York or nineteenth-century London, it doesn't always pay to be too 'precious' for one's art.

A PROPER CHARLIE
KNIGHTSBRIDGE CROWN COURT, LONDON, 1981

It might be considered unfair to label Judge Sir Harold Cassel the leading exponent of verbal judicial gaffery. But then he did put his foot in it in rather a spectacular fashion. For the 'Proper Charlie' epithet that became his in 1981 was one entirely of his own making. The press merely reported the facts.

In the interests of lightening the burden of embarrassment, though, let him share this bench of mirth and shame with other master exponents of the 'I wish I hadn't said that' breed.

First up, though, is the man himself. At Knightsbridge Crown Court on Wednesday, 19 August 1981, Sir Harold was presiding over the trial of 27-year-old Alexander Steel from Balham, who was facing three charges of burglary.

Judge Cassel was full of bonhomie that day. As the court adjourned for lunch he did a remarkable thing. Despite a warning by police that it might be unwise, he granted the prisoner an hour's bail to go and have some lunch. Conscious that there was a vital element of trust implicit in this temporary grant of freedom, Judge Cassel looked Steel straight in the eye and uttered those famous last words: 'Be sure to come back. If you don't you will make me look a proper Charlie.'

With barely disguised delight the next day's *Times* reported in deadpan fashion: 'Last night police were still looking for

Mr Steel.' There have been plenty of jailbreaks for freedom but this unique lunchbreak for freedom dogged Sir Harold Cassel, the self-christened 'Proper Charlie', from that day on.

Mercifully, he can take comfort that he is not alone. From across the Atlantic comes the booming voice of a New York judge who in 1985 was formally admonished for commenting, as a female advocate entered his courtroom, 'What a set of knockers!'

Again from the States, but rather more sinister, was the response of the judge in a 1970s trial to the request of a lawyer of Japanese extraction that he be given more time to prepare his case: 'How much time did you give us at Pearl Harbor?' wasn't exactly a polite rebuff.

Nor do Americans have a monopoly on such indiscretions. On 30 September 1992 at Hereford Crown Court, 65-year-old Judge John Lee incurred the not inconsiderable wrath of British womanhood during the trial of 20-year-old Robert Ward.

Ward's crime was a hold-up at a solicitor's office, and he explained to the court that he wanted to be arrested to escape from troubles with his girlfriend.

Judge Lee, in passing a lenient sentence of two years' probation, told the defendant, 'So you've had problems with women. Who do you think hasn't? It's part of a woman's function in life to upset men.' When asked later by a female reporter to explain his remarks, the judge further fanned the flames by barking the riposte: 'Which lesbian group are you from?'

In fairness to such exponents of bench buffoonery it ought to be said that some of their most publicised boobs are born entirely from ignorance rather than malice. During the famous *Oz* obscenity trial in 1971, Judge Argyle needed to ask, 'What is *Hair*?' at a time when the famous nude rock musical was plastered all over the papers. And in 1979 Mr Justice Cantley heard a case relating to the ban imposed on a former England football manager by the Football Association. Midway through hearing the testimony of various players he turned to a barrister and asked, 'Kevin Keegan, does he play for England or Scotland?'

Popular music runs sport a close second in the list of subjects inclined to befuddle the judiciary: 'Who is Bruce Springsteen?' from Mr Justice Harman in 1985 might almost seem credible, but 'Who are the Rolling Stones?' from a Canadian judge trying Keith Richards for possession of heroin in 1977 must be regarded as a corker by any standards.

Yet where would we be without such classics? The legal world is more entertaining for these occasional gaffes, some of which have survived many years after their originators have experienced their own final judgment.

Let's give the last word to the Manchester judge presiding in the 1920s at a case in which two young offenders had committed mutual indecency in one of the city's WCs. He told the court in passing sentence, 'The public lavatories of Manchester have got to be cleaned up and I propose to make a start.' Not content with that he finished by saying, 'You two men have to take yourselves in hand and pull yourselves together.'

How would our learned judges respond if asked to comment on such classic bloopers?

That's an easy one – 'What is a blooper?'

EIGHT OUT OF TEN CATS PREFER HILDA

STONEHAM, MASSACHUSETTS, UNITED STATES, 1982

Many barbarous acts have been discovered by the police in the line of routine duty. Even the vilest sights have to be met with a dispassionate heart and sound stomach. Yet once in a while even the most hardened officer is shocked by how a victim has been treated by an attacker. Such was a nasty-tasting case that comes from the USA.

Hilda Diggdon was one of those delightfully eccentric old ladies who like to take in stray cats. No one knew exactly how many she had but it was certainly a lot. If there was an abandoned moggy in need of a home she couldn't resist it.

Nor could the cats resist Hilda. Maybe they used their psychic powers to spread the word, for the Diggdon home became a magnet for fallen felines from miles around.

Alas her guests may have had nine lives but Hilda enjoyed only one. Late in 1982 her remains were discovered on the floor of her home. She was 84. 'The body was in a semi-skeletal state,' a police officer confirmed. 'It was one of the roughest things I've ever seen.'

The work of a homicidal maniac on a particularly imaginative day? In fact not, for the autopsy revealed that Hilda had died of natural causes.

Yet even in death she had remained irresistible to her feline friends: not being adept at opening the tins of food that remained in the kitchen cupboard, they had bitten the hand that had fed them – and the foot, and the leg and the neck, until very little remained of Hilda at all.

'They were feeding off her and when we tried to recover the body they attacked us,' said one of the officers who made the gruesome find.

Time was when misbehaving animals could face trial (see 'The Accused Have Gone to Ground'). In Savigny, France, on 10 January 1457, a sow which had trampled on a five-year-old boy was charged and convicted of 'murder flagrantly committed on the person of Jehan Martin' and sentenced to be 'hanged by the hind feet to a gallows tree'.

But Hilda's cats hadn't murdered. Perhaps their more considered act was even worse. Did they all partake of the tainted morsels or do some cats have a conscience? In the event the authorities took no chances. All the cats were removed and their lives humanely ended.

But just think of the squeals of that poor medieval swine hanging from its gibbet. By comparison some would say that a swift injection was too good an end for the most ghoulish cats in legal history.

ONE CASE TOO MANY

RAMSGATE MAGISTRATES' COURT, 1983

Judges aren't generally too fussy about which cases they handle. Large or small, it's all part of the job. But there was one case that 67-year-old Judge Bruce Campbell really shouldn't have touched. In December 1983 it made legal history to his own personal cost after proceedings in the unlikely setting of Ramsgate Magistrates' Court.

The case he handled was no ordinary case. A large one? A small one? A quick one? It might have been any, for this was a case of whisky. In fact several cases. And some cigarettes. Oh, dear. The crime of smuggling may be redolent of long-ago moonlit nights on which gnarled old sailor types rowed silently into secluded coves, but Judge Campbell seemed intent on carrying the tradition into the modern era.

His frequent journeys to Guernsey in his motor cruiser *Papyrus* aroused the interest of the vigilant men and women from HM Customs after a tip-off from a public-spirited citizen of Ramsgate. When officers raided the vessel they found the small matter of 125 litres (28 gallons) of whisky and 9,000 cigarettes, which Campbell had brought over from the Channel Islands with his friend Alan Foreman, a market trader and second-hand car dealer.

Imagine the conversation: 'Have you come to a decision, Mr Foreman?' 'Yes, I'll do it.'

Even a well-practised judge couldn't explain away those amounts of booze and fags on the basis of 'personal use' and at Ramsgate Magistrates' Court in September 1982 Judge Bruce Campbell QC was convicted and fined £2,000.

There was bound to be fallout from such an unusual case and it was Campbell who fell and Campbell who was out. On Monday, 5 December 1983 he received a punishment never before meted out to an English judge in modern times when he was unceremoniously removed from office by the Lord Chancellor, Lord Hailsham, under the Courts Act of 1971.

Suitably humiliated by the scandal, ex-Judge Campbell retreated with his tail between his legs to his country home in Thames Ditton. There he pondered the loss of his £29,750 salary, his pension rights and the nice little flat in the Temple. This smear on the face of British justice might be hard to bear for ardent traditionalists, but it's comforting to note that judges from across the Atlantic are inclined to go one 'better'.

In 1999 the Supreme Court of Mississippi removed Howard 'Buster' Spencer from his position as a judge in Prentiss County for a string of inappropriate acts including swearing at witnesses and lawyers and continually sucking lollipops in court.

But Judge Spencer's behaviour was exemplary compared with that of Richard Deacon Jones of Omaha, Nebraska. He was dismissed in 1998, again for displaying a variety of unusual behaviour patterns, not least signing important court papers 'Adolf Hitler', setting bail bonds for 'a zillion dollars', and throwing lighted fireworks into a rival colleague's office before urinating on the carpet. His fate was ultimately sealed after he promised the authorities that the Hitler business would stop – it did, but alas he started signing court papers 'Snow White' instead.

Surely a spot of 'gentleman' smuggling is almost admirable after that. So when it comes to the strange world of judges behaving badly, raising a glass to Bruce Campbell might not be too inappropriate after all.

INNOCENT OF AN IMPOSSIBLE CRIME

THE HOUSE OF LORDS, LONDON, 1985

One of the fundamental tenets of the British justice system is the right of appeal to a higher authority. Some cases go all the way to be heard by representatives of the House of Lords.

Naturally, because they are extremely busy fellows, the Lords will only consent to pass final judgment on the really 'big' cases and there is a rigorous prescreening process to check that only the most important ones get through.

Thus it was that on Thursday, 9 May 1985, a pivotal day for the future of British justice, five Law Lords exercised their razor-sharp intellects to decide the fate of Mrs Bernadette Ryan of Manchester in the case of the nicked video recorder.

I feel an explanation, dear reader, is required.

Having paid £110 for the video recorder, Mrs Ryan was unhappy when it was stolen in a burglary from her home. She reported the incident to police but during the course of questioning the plot began to thicken: 'I might as well be honest,' she told police, 'it was a stolen one I bought.' A curious brand of honesty ...

That admission was Mrs Ryan's first 'mistake', which later proved an error in more ways than one.

Under the Theft Act 1968 and the Criminal Attempt Act 1981 she was promptly charged with 'dishonestly handling a video recorder contrary to the 1968 Act knowing or believing it to be stolen and dishonestly attempting to handle that recorder contrary to section 1 (1) of the 1981 Act'.

In a prosecution by James Anderton, Chief Constable of Greater Manchester, Mrs Ryan pleaded not guilty to both charges. It was when the court heard details of her second 'mistake' that things got more interesting, for it turned out that her belief that her video was a stolen one was erroneous. Or at least the prosecution couldn't prove it was stolen. This presented something of a conundrum and as a consequence Greater Manchester Police dropped the first charge of dishonest handling of stolen goods but invited magistrates instead simply to convict her of dishonest 'attempted' handling under the 1981 Act.

This was where the 1981 Act should have scored, for the government had brought it in largely to secure convictions against criminals who cited the age-old 'pickpocket's defence': 'All right officer, you caught me with my hand in his pocket but the pocket was empty so how can you accuse me of attempted theft?' The 1981 Act quashed the validity of such spurious defences by making provision for convictions against those attempting a 'hypothetically impossible crime'.

Bernadette Ryan was undoubtedly guilty of 'attempted handling of stolen goods' under that interpretation of the Act even though she only 'believed' the goods to be stolen. She had tried to commit the 'impossible crime' but the court in Manchester perversely found her innocent.

This potentially gave leave to all manner of strange acquittal scenarios. Consider a man brutally stabbing his wife while she lies 'asleep' in bed. But a doctor later testifies she had already died some hours earlier from a heart attack. Under *Ryan v. Anderton* the husband must duly be acquitted of 'attempted' murder. Consider another scenario – a jealous wife plunges a carving knife deep into her husband's chest as he lies in bed under the covers. It turns out he has nipped out to see his lover and left only a bolster in his place. The wife is guilty of nothing more than stabbing a pillow and again walks free.

Conscious of the can of worms the *Anderton v. Ryan* case might open up, the Divisional Court subsequently ordered the Manchester court that they must convict Mrs Ryan, but the handler of the sham stolen goods had by this time become truly convinced of her own innocence. She went to the top.

It was entirely to be expected that the Law Lords would back up the government's 1981 legislation and find Bernadette Ryan guilty. But in *The Law's Strangest Cases* the only thing to expect with any certainty is the unexpected. They found Mrs Ryan innocent of the charge on a vote of four to one and therefore allowed her appeal.

The Times somewhat incredulously wrote of the decision that 'on 9 May 1985 the Law Lords drove a coach and horses through the Government's 1981 Criminal Attempt Act'.

This strange affair set the philosophers of the legal world buzzing with what-ifs: 'What if a man steals a briefcase full of waste paper when he really believes it to contain £20,000?' poses one. 'Under the 1981 Act he ought to be guilty of attempted theft of £20,000' says the second. 'But after the Ryan acquittal all he can be found guilty of is stealing the waste paper,' chips in a third. 'And the briefcase,' pipes a pedantic but quite correct fourth.

So there is the odd affair of *Anderton v. Ryan*, which goes to show that sometimes the smallest cases can become the biggest. It doesn't pay, though, to spend too much time pondering the mind-boggling permutations of this one, as an exploding brain is not a pleasant experience.

One final thought though. The most astonishing facet of this case is surely that Bernadette Ryan should have had the bare-faced cheek to report the 'burglary' of goods she believed she had dishonestly acquired in the first place.

Would you invite the law into your home in those circumstances? Now that really is strange.

IT'S UNCLE NORRIS!
THE HIGH COURT, LONDON, 1986

Libel is a strange business. The traditional test for spotting one is whether the words written or spoken bring a person into hatred, ridicule or contempt. That's a difficult one to call and more recent thinking has suggested that an approach better suited to modern life would be 'to determine whether the words lower a person in the estimation of right-thinking people'.

Could anything be simpler? Differential calculus or the translation of Serbo-Croat into Japanese come to mind, for the history of libel cases shows that a person can be libelled not only by the written and spoken word but also by image, theme and juxtaposition. The possibilities are endless and in truth it's all a bit of a minefield, but one that any legal strangeologist is more than happy to negotiate because oddities are guaranteed.

Take the 1975 case of *Cosmos Air Holidays v. BBC*. For the BBC to tell their *Holiday* programme viewers that some hotels used by Cosmos weren't up to scratch might just have been bearable to the tour company's bosses but it was the accompanying music that really got their goat. They settled for several thousand pounds in out of court damages – after all, how else could the viewers interpret the opening music of the *Colditz* television series? There was no escape for the BBC at any rate – it was libel by theme, literally.

As for libel by juxtaposition, look no further than Mr

Monson, who, even as far back as 1894, was sufficiently litigation-aware to get himself all worked up about the waxwork of himself that Madame Tussaud's placed in the anteroom of their Chamber of Horrors. Monson *had* been tried for murder in a Scottish court, it was true, but he had equally certainly been acquitted by that peculiar Scottish verdict of 'not proven'. To place his likeness next to those of convicted murderers just wasn't on, he argued, and he won the princely sum of one farthing's damages for having his reputation sullied in such a way.

And then there's image. Here we come to the star of the show. I give you Norris McWhirter, respected editor of the *Guinness Book of Records*, no less.

Perhaps he was trying to get into his own book for the shortest and most tenuous incidence of libel of all time. Or maybe he'd just lost his sense of humour.

It all started with the television broadcast of a 1984 episode of *Spitting Image*, the series whose lampoonery through the medium of cruelly parodic puppetry has caused many a celebrity to fume.

The good news for Norris was that he wasn't on it. Or was he? For thereby hangs the tale.

The Times subsequently reported that Mr McWhirter, aged 59, had taken out an action for libel against the Independent Broadcasting Authority at Horseferry Road Magistrates' Court. McWhirter was adamant that he had seen 'a grotesque and ridiculing image of my face superimposed on the top of a body of a naked woman'. It really doesn't bear thinking about. He asserted that the broadcasting of the image was a criminal offence under the Broadcasting Act 1981, but not because of 'what' it was – it was how long it lasted that was the real bone of contention.

'And how long did it last?' asked the judge with due concern. Norris McWhirter's reply was brief but not nearly as brief as the offending image: 'A quarter of a second,' was his stunning reply.

McWhirter's contention was that the image had been broadcast subliminally, using the sort of technique that unscrupulous advertisers or political regimes are said to employ to implant subconscious images and messages into the addled brains of the world's couch potatoes.

This wasn't the sort of case to be decided in the blink of an eye, and so to the High Court on Thursday, 30 January 1986, where Lord Justice Lloyd, sitting in the Queen's Bench Divisional Court with Mr Justice Skinner, held Norris McWhirter's reputation in his hands.

Lord Justice Lloyd asked the question that any person in the street would have asked: 'If the image was only on screen for a quarter of a second how did you see it?'

That was where the evidence of Mr McWhirter's 15-year-old nephew came into its own: 'He was watching the programme on video using the slow-motion,' said McWhirter, 'and when he used the freeze-frame button he suddenly shouted "Look, there's Uncle Norris!"'

Unconcerned as to why the teenager should have been using the freeze-frame in the first place (perusing naked women?), Lord Justice Lloyd remained singularly unimpressed, promptly quashing the summons and prohibiting further proceedings.

Thus it was that Norris McWhirter failed to get into the *Guinness Book of Records* and he was left to bemoan the verdict, leaving the court with an impassioned parting shot: 'This is a matter of profound constitutional importance,' he said. 'This brainwashing should be suppressed – these subliminal messages are deceitful and I want them stopped.'

Has there ever been an odder libel case? Probably not – and there is a lesson we can all learn from Uncle Norris. Never feel guilty about reaching for that extra biscuit while watching television. Just blame those subliminal messages and sue.

NOT SO DUMB WITNESS

SOUTHAMPTON, 1987

It seems rather unfair that the 'Queen of Crime' Agatha Christie should have titled her 1937 novel *Dumb Witness*; Bob the dog, the witness referred to, was undoubtedly devoid of speech but certainly not stupid in the sense that 'dumb' has come to convey.

Indeed the idea of a dog, or indeed any creature, as an articulate witness is an appealing one. But animals only talk in literature and film. Like the rabbits in *Watership Down*.

Thereby hangs a curious link. For in Southampton in 1987 the author of that very book, David Adams, scored a major hit for the anthropomorphic lobby. He called his dog Tetter as a witness in an industrial tribunal case involving the unsavoury antics of a gun-toting gamekeeper.

It was late summer 1985 when Adams and Tetter went walking on a public footpath near Whitchurch, Hampshire, close to the area Adams used as the inspiration for his book.

There he encountered David Hunt, head gamekeeper on an estate at nearby Middleton to Captain Andrew Wills of the famous tobacco family.

There was not a whiff of trouble in the air that day but gamekeeper Hunt, not known for his sentimentality towards rabbits, or humans for that matter, seemed to be spoiling for a confrontation.

Spotting that Tetter wasn't on a lead, he launched into a fierce verbal tirade, turning the air a shade too deep a blue for Adams's liking. Nor did Hunt altogether endear himself to the multi-award-winning author when he finished off with 'You're the one who wrote that poxy book about rabbits.'

Shots were fired. Tetter was threatened but not hit and Adams had nightmares about the incident for months afterwards. Yet it was entirely by coincidence that he was able to gain a measure of redress and clear Tetter's name from Hunt's scandalous accusation that he had been 'out of control and scattered my pheasants'.

It seems Hunt's volatile temper also affected his fellow employees, for his assistant David Claridge was so unnerved by the unpredictability of the outbursts that he quit his job. It was a job he otherwise enjoyed and as a result he sued his employer Andrew Wills for constructive dismissal. That case went to an industrial tribunal in January 1987.

Adams was called as a witness to testify to the ferocity of Hunt's temper. He told the hearing how the gamekeeper used language that was 'a celebration of filth' before firing his shotgun in Tetter's direction: 'I thought he had shot my dog dead,' said Adams.

Hunt's defence was that Tetter was uncontrollable. But Adams assured the tribunal that Tetter would obey his every command, even in strange surroundings. There was only one thing for it. 'Call Tetter.'

The dog's big moment came on 27 January 1987. This rare canine witness even made the pages of *The Times*, the reporter wrote:

'The dog bounded into the tribunal room. But when Mr Adams commanded it to sit, it did so instantly.'

In a scene reminiscent of the best *Lassie* episodes, Tetter had won the day. His reputation remained unsullied and Andrew Wills agreed to pay Claridge £2,000. It is to be hoped that Tetter was rewarded with a tasty morsel or two.

Lest I should be accused of canine bias I must continue the theme with the 1983 case of 'Blackie the Talking Cat'. Blackie was a variation on the age-old music hall acts of animals that give responses to certain questions posed by their owners. But Blackie's business status had got his keepers into a spot of bother regarding the imposition of a business-licence tax.

Their desire not to pay it led the case to go all the way to the US Court of Appeals. There was much talk of 'animal rights' and 'free speech'. But the result for Blackie was something of a humiliation, as the court asserted that 'even if an animal could enjoy such rights we see no reason for the appellants to assert them for him as Blackie can clearly speak for himself'. Touché for Blackie, who dismally failed to respond.

That begs the final question of how disadvantaged animals might truly assert themselves in this unfair law business.

The special 'dog court' set up in 1979 in Multnomah County Court, Portland, Oregon, sounds like a good start and it created enough canine-related business to keep a judge occupied for one day a week.

Heartening, too, is another US case, this one involving Bimbo the performing elephant. In 1972 a Los Angeles judge, Justice Title, awarded Bimbo's owners $4,500 as a result of injuries received by the elephant in a road accident. Justice Title accepted that since the accident 'Bimbo has completely lost interest in dancing and water skiing'.

It is to England, though, that we should look for action of a more direct and graphic kind. The teenagers who attacked a woman in Dalton, near Huddersfield, and snatched her plastic bag got nothing but soiled goods – the poop-scoop contents left by her pet terrier. Specimen charges were later preferred.

But the final word goes to the feline world and a symbolic act which struck at the very heart of English justice.

On 22 March 1979, an unnamed cat made its views on

matters legal all too clear. *The Daily Telegraph* reported in admirably deadpan style: 'Proceedings at the Old Bailey were delayed for 15 minutes while the court was disinfected owing to a cat's misdemeanour.'

THE ICING ON THE CAKE
BELFAST, NORTHERN IRELAND, 1988

As strange libel cases go, this one certainly takes the biscuit. 1988 may have been a year of much more important cases than *Boal and McCartney v. the Sunday World* but as far as the legal community of Belfast was concerned it was the tastiest morsel to come their way for many a year.

For once, the public gallery at Belfast's High Court was patronised not by a handful of curious onlookers but tightly packed instead by an audience of barristers, solicitors and court officials relishing the prospect of the bun fight of the year as the case opened in October 1988.

Bringing the action, as plaintiffs, not lawyers, were the two best-known QCs in Northern Ireland, the leading criminal barrister Desmond Boal and the top civil QC and Unionist politician Robert McCartney.

The action centred not on some complex legal ruling but on the much simpler and far more entertaining matter of chocolate eclairs, or rather alleged chocolate eclairs, for the plaintiffs were to claim in the strongest possible terms that said cream-filled confections were entirely illusory.

It was a freelance journalist writing in the Dublin-based *Sunday World* newspaper who started it all. In 1987 the paper ran his piece headed WHO NEARLY HAD A BUN-FIGHT?, which informed its amused readers that the two eminent QCs had entered a bakery shop both intent on buying chocolate eclairs.

'Unfortunately,' said the piece, 'there were very few left and some other shoppers were amazed as the two "had words" about who saw them first.'

Boal and McCartney were not amused by the story and Boal's QC, Michael Lavery, was at pains to tell the court that the report was 'pure garbage' and that 'my client has been held to ridicule'. If the evidence of the smirking ranks of Belfast's legal community was anything to go by it seems he may have had a point. The courtroom abounded with much undisguised mirth.

Mr McCartney's evidence was no less forgiving: 'When you have put as much effort as I have into achieving a position as a respected, I hope, and respectable QC, then to be portrayed in a totally pernicious and lying article as some form of contemptible and senseless clown who would make an exhibition of himself in a bakery shop made me very distressed and very angry.'

Those strong denials were all very well but the question that all in court must have been pondering was why a journalist should choose two legal heavyweights as his comic characters in a fabricated tale. How, too, could he possibly have had the imagination to create the chocolate-eclair affair? Surely there's no smoke without fire?

The answers duly came when the evidence for the *Sunday World* was presented. When pressed on the point they readily admitted that the incident had never occurred. There was no shop, no encounter between the two QCs and no chocolate eclairs. The freelance journalist responsible for the entire confection said from the witness box, 'I thought it was true at the time and it was only a trivial humorous item.'

Trivial and humorous it may have been to him but the two QCs sought substantial damages. It seems the *Sunday World* had made an unwise editorial decision in picking on the legal bigwigs, for damages were duly awarded. And this was no 1p-each case.

Blessedly Boal and McCartney received exactly equal shares in the rather mouth-watering award, as the *Sunday World* paid out for the most expensive eclairs, or alleged eclairs, in history. The two QCs received £50,000 each.

THE MOST DESPERATE APPEAL EVER

SONORA, CALIFORNIA, UNITED STATES, 1988

No lawyer likes losing a case but, unless there are good grounds for an appeal, taking it on the chin is the only truly professional way to handle such hazards of the job.

But meek acceptance just wasn't the way for a US defence attorney, Clarke Head, who risked being labelled a windy loser as he launched the most spurious appeal in legal history.

Head's client at the trial in Sonora, California, in December 1988, faced a tough prospect. Thirty-seven-year-old Gary Davenport was charged with five counts of felony and one misdemeanour stemming from a break-in at a state highway maintenance yard in September 1986.

The prosecuting lawyer, Assistant District Attorney Ned Lowenbach, presented a forceful case against Davenport. All Clarke Head could do was brace himself for one last effort in defence of his client in his closing speech.

Meanwhile Lowenbach was also bracing himself for an effort of a different kind, one he hoped might serve as a silent but deadly sabotage of his opponent's eloquence. But, if Head's subsequent accusations were to be believed, the attack was more in the way of a foul and noisy quickfire.

AN ILL WIND IN COURT BRINGS GALES OF LAUGHTER, said the *Independent*'s headline of 14 December. Gary Davenport had been unsurprisingly convicted on six counts but Clarke Head announced his intention to appeal on the grounds of 'gross misconduct' on the part of Lowenbach.

'The closing speech is supposed to be sacred,' he complained. 'It's like the defendant's last chance and you aren't supposed to interrupt, especially making the jury laugh like Lowenbach did.' It was a curious statement to make because, according to Mr Head, Ned Lowenbach had spoken only once during the closing speech and that was to mutter a rather sheepish 'sorry' through tightly clenched teeth.

Head further explained: 'During my closing speech Lowenbach farted about a hundred times and made the jury laugh. He claims it was an accident but I don't think it was. He just kept on doing it to show his disrespect for me, my case and my client. He continually moved around and then he would fart again. I've been through 50 jury trials and never heard anything like this. It was impossible to concentrate.'

It is a toss-up which is more astonishing. The utter desperation of the grounds of the appeal itself or the possibility that anyone could really achieve the magic century entirely at will. District Attorney Eric Du Temple immediately defended his assistant: 'We are not going to dignify this with a response,' he sniffed.

The end result of this unseemly spat was that there was no let-off for Davenport but eyebrows were certainly raised on this side of the Atlantic as a senior member of the Bar Council was moved to remark, 'I know of no barristers being accused of similar behaviour in a British court. The difference between acceptable courtroom conduct in Britain and America is quite marked.'

One must wonder what became of the only alleged serial flatulator in legal history, but an alternative career as a novel variety act must surely have been his for the taking in the land where the law and the ass are now for ever inextricably linked.

DUMB WITNESS
CARDIFF CROWN COURT, 1989

The law concerning the right of an accused person to maintain absolute silence when questioned is undeniably complex. That has encouraged rather than deterred generations of suspects to say, 'I am saying nothing', which, despite its being rather a contradiction in terms, has put a spanner in the works on many occasions.

At times like this a persuasive judge or barrister might coax such a silent witness into opening up, but at Cardiff Crown Court on Friday, 19 May 1989, Patricia Morgan was taking no such chances of breaking her silence.

The charges against Ms Morgan were of the all-too-familiar kind, namely defrauding the Department of Social Security by obtaining £9,000 in benefit payments via false claims.

She denied the charges and as her cross-examination was about to begin she made it clear to Judge Michael Evans QC that her lips were sealed. This she achieved by passing a note to him, which read: 'Your Honour, I Patricia Morgan have superglued my mouth to draw the public's attention to the mistrial and injustice of this court.' The note further alleged that a police tape-recorded interview with Ms Morgan had been tampered with.

Not having encountered such a determined silence before, Judge Evans sent out the jury and pondered the next move. Ms Morgan, from Newport, Gwent, was taken to hospital with her lips firmly stuck together and returned to the dock three hours later apparently none the worse for her experience.

Judge Evans announced to the jury, 'Ms Morgan is now back with us and her mouth has been unstopped,' before adjourning the case until the following Monday, when the silent lady finally came unstuck.

Further to the theme of silence in court, it may be the accused who most often favour that stance, but on at least one occasion the tables were well and truly turned when the Judiciary had *their* say – or not, as the case may be.

It was in Paris on 18 February 1971 that all proceedings in the Palace of Justice were suspended for the afternoon when judges responded to recent criticism by leading political figures that they 'lacked courage' by holding a silent vigil. *The Times* reported that 'all the judges held an impressive demonstration, moving impassively through the long corridors of the Palace in complete silence'.

There was on that occasion not even a smidgeon of glue involved, but nor was any needed, for, as everybody knows, judges under criticism are inclined to stick together.

THE SHOCKING AFFAIR OF THE ROLLED UMBRELLA

THE OLD BAILEY, LONDON, 1990

Every right-thinking judge and all upright members of the public want justice to be seen to be done. But at any price? Now there's the rub, for trials cost money, and public money at that. That's why judges and the public occasionally raise an eyebrow over cases they consider to be 'a waste of time and money'.

Take Judge Abdela in August 1981: 'Yes, it was true that Anthony Luckie had underpaid his tube fare by 85 pence,' he said, as he fined the unemployed 24-year-old £50, 'but why am I hearing this case at the Central Criminal Court over two days at a cost of £4,000 when it should have been dealt with routinely at Kingston?'

Judge Abdela was not really interested in the answer, that is that the Old Bailey generally helps to clear the summer backlog from London's crown courts. What he was really demanding was that 'this should never ever happen again'.

He might have known better, for cases of this type habitually occur year after year. Many would qualify for *The Law's Strangest Cases* but selectivity calls and it is my duty to make the pick of the bunch. With that in mind let's drop in at a petrol station in Hackney, east London, in the summer of 1990.

Keith Gonaz, aged 31, was topping up his car with petrol. He had a £10 note in his pocket ready to pay for the £10 worth of fuel he intended to put in, but, like many motorists before and since, he found that self-service can be a little tricky. His nozzle control, in particular, needed some fine tuning and he accidentally overshot the mark by 2p. 'It was a hair-trigger reaction,' he pleaded to the cashier. 'I tried to stop it but it was too late.' Many drivers will sympathise.

Mr Gonaz consequently refused to pay the additional 2p but the cashier remained entirely unmoved and insisted on the 2p payment forthwith.

A momentary impasse and verbal spat ensued but Mr Gonaz was determined not to budge. In a good-humoured but arguably puerile effort to defuse the situation he pointed his rolled umbrella at the cashier, made a machine-gun noise and drove off. The 'jobsworth' cashier promptly pressed the (aptly named in this case) panic button and the police rounded up the dangerous desperado just a few minutes later.

Again, owing to a backlog at the lesser courts, the case came to the Old Bailey, where there was sufficient capacity to hear it. Shouldn't their publicity department have been drumming up some more serious crimes? 'Ever fancied trying your hand at murder? Give it a go. We need the business' has a certain ring to it.

As it was, Friday, 7 December 1990 was a day when Judge Bruce Laughland QC must have wondered what all his years of training were really for as the charges against Gonaz were read out.

That the incident should have given rise to formal charges of 'failure to discharge a debt of 2p, affray, and threatening behaviour' seemed rather over the top, but the real *coup de grâce* was 'possessing an imitation firearm' – to wit, the rolled umbrella.

As the judge ordered not-guilty verdicts to be entered on the firearm and affray charges, and the jury found Gonaz not guilty on the count of threatening behaviour, his mood displayed no sign of fitting his name. 'Laughland'? Not exactly.

'This has been a two-day case,' he concluded at the end of the farcical proceedings, 'and I should point out that each court costs at least £25 a minute to run, not including counsel and solicitors' fees. Pursuing this matter and holding a trial by jury was an unjustified waste of public time and money and will cost the taxpayer at least £13,500.'

He was absolutely right of course, and concluded in the standard manner: 'This must never be allowed to happen again.' Judge Laughland had spoken and he expected his words to be heeded. That being the case any subsequent reports you may have read about three youths being cleared of stealing two cans of lager costing £1.80 in a trial at the Old Bailey costing the taxpayer an estimated £131,000 must be purely a figment of your imagination. That is your imagination in June 1998 by the way.

Where will it all end? With such evil criminals at large there will be no let-up at the Old Bailey, that's for sure. Why, only the other day I experienced at first hand the terror that now stalks our streets as I was the victim of an attempted gang murder just yards from my home. A party of elderly ladies disgorging from a bus trip bore down on me with indisputably merciless intentions, for without exception they were carrying rolled umbrellas.

AN UNEXPECTED STRETCH

THE OLD BAILEY, LONDON, 1992

Wilfred and Peggy Harte lived a quiet enough life at their maisonette in Walworth, southeast London. With Tweek the budgie they made a cosy threesome, but then Peggy's relatives came calling.

That was Wilf's first bit of bad luck and he was soon to find that he was in for a stretch of it. It was a run of ill-fortune that led the 61-year-old straight to the Old Bailey.

When four of the in-laws arrived for a three-day visit he took a deep breath and determined to smile his way through. When they decided to stay for an extra day his spirits sagged. When that stretched to another day he got a bit twitchy and longed to hear those four little words that all the best-loved relatives time to perfection.

Alas, Peggy's tribe mastered 'What's on the telly?' with ease but seemed to encounter untold difficulty with the much more resonant 'We'll get our coats.' By the time the three days had stretched to three weeks Wilf wondered whether the unwanted guests would ever leave. His wife, though, was loving the company and when three weeks became three months Wilf was near the end of his tether.

At his trial at the Old Bailey in November 1992 he relived the torment for the benefit of the jury: 'I felt they'd taken over my life,' he said. 'They watched television until five in the morning. My electric bill doubled and I paid the rent, poll tax and all the other bills on top. I got the idea they were permanently settled so I decided to do something drastic.'

Wilf's version of drastic was five gallons of petrol poured on the floors while the aliens slept. After he had first made sure that Tweek the budgie was safe, a single match did the rest.

The court heard that it was amazing good fortune that nobody was seriously hurt. Wilf's arrest had swiftly followed and he told police, 'It was a good blaze. I feel euphoric.'

He had little choice but to admit the charge of reckless arson and was inevitably found guilty. No doubt Wilf felt he'd already served a three-month sentence but more was to come as he was jailed for three and a half years.

When asked if he had anything to say his response went unrecorded – but it probably wasn't 'Will I be allowed visitors?'

A KNIFE-AND-FORK JOB
LINCOLN CROWN COURT, 1992

When Allison Johnson arrived at Lincoln Crown Court on 24 August 1992 accused of aggravated burglary, it wasn't his first time. In fact the 47-year-old had already spent a total of 24 years in jail, so getting off this time round didn't look likely.

True to form he was found guilty of breaking into two homes and threatening the residents with a knife. He was promptly sentenced to four years. Yet it wasn't because of his choice of weapon that Johnson was known as 'the cutlery man', for during the trial the open-mouthed court heard evidence of his unique brand of stealing silverware.

The prosecution were at pains to point out that the accused had stolen knives, forks and spoons at countless restaurants – by swallowing them! The loot was invariably washed down with liberal quantities of something strong. He favoured beer over Brasso.

This remarkably strange habit had landed Johnson in the operating theatre even more times than he'd been sent down. At the last count he'd been under the knife no fewer than 30 times to remove pieces of cutlery from his stomach.

Adrian Robinson, for the defence, sought the sympathy vote: 'My client still has eight forks lodged in his stomach and has only been given a year to live,' he said. 'The cutlery-swallowing-and-alcohol habit comes from his lack of self-esteem.'

The jury were evidently neither moved nor amused as they duly pronounced him guilty. But at least one report of the trial saw the humorous side of this rather tragic case: 'As Johnson was led away he was clearly rattled.'

THE ACCUSED IS FREE TO CROW

BIDEFORD, 1992

Such was the high feeling surrounding a case heard at Bideford, Devon, on 11 May 1992 that almost an entire community turned up in court to back the accused.

The idyllic little village of Stoke had only 27 houses, yet 54 of its residents hired a coach to descend on Bideford to cheer on their local favourite. That unprecedented ratio of support was all the more remarkable for the fact that the dastardly villain of the piece was a cockerel named Corky.

This unusual town-versus-country battle started in November 1991 when a 'townie', John Ritchings, moved to the village and complained about Corky's early-morning crowing. Much to the irritation of the long-standing locals, he successfully obtained a noise-abatement order from Torridge District Council and poor old Corky was forced to move from the cosy home he shared with 14 hens to a life of solitary confinement in a distant converted conservatory.

Corky's owner, Margery Johns, was outraged. Nor was Corky overly impressed. The village was duly mobilised and an appeal launched. The Sunday before the case came to court even the vicar pleaded clemency for Corky as he addressed the issue in his sermon.

Jeremy Ferguson for Mrs Johns was brief and to the point: 'This is a case of town versus country, pure and simple, and we say Corky is simply doing his natural duty. You shouldn't complain about country noises in the country.'

Mr Ritchings, cast in the guise of Public Enemy Number One, was eloquent in his assertion that Corky woke him up far too early and, as a consequence, had caused him to suffer ever-mounting nervous tension.

But Corky knew all about mounting tension too, and Mrs Johns spoke passionately in her cockerel's favour. So passionately that the drama proved all too much for her – she suffered a fainting fit after giving evidence.

Corky himself did not appear but waited anxiously, now henless for fully six months, back in the village.

He might almost have heard the cheers as the magistrate, David Quance, overturned the abatement order, but Mr Ritchings, clutching a file 2in (5cm) thick on what had become to him a battle royal, vowed to fight on.

Thus it was that a county court judge in Barnstaple was put on the spot a week later to pass final judgment. There was good news and bad news. The bad news for Corky was that he was confined to his second home from 10p.m. to 8a.m. on Monday to Thursday and 10p.m. to 3p.m. Friday to Sunday. But the long-awaited good news was that he was free to join his hens during the day.

He was soon reported to be enjoying himself immensely, making up for lost time. John Ritchings may have got his lie-in but Corky, the accused with the best court following of all time, was certainly crowing the louder.

A SYMBOLIC CRIME
CARDIFF COUNTY COURT, 1992

Some respected authorities on the folklore of the legal system have asserted that the real authority of a judge or barrister comes not from his mastery of the law, or his pin-sharp mental faculties and incisive use of language, but from his wig.

Some eminent legal commentators have gone to pains to elucidate the vulnerability of a wigless judge, none more pointedly than Judge H.C. Leon (1902–76), perhaps better known by his writing pen name Henry Cecil: 'A judge complained that he had to share the same lavatory as the litigants and witnesses,' he wrote in 1970. 'But many people who have seen a judge in court do not recognise him without his wig. And it is highly undesirable, in my view, that the judge standing next to a man in the lavatory should have the opportunity of hearing himself described as a "cock-eyed old so-and-so".'

Over a century before, in 1841, Charles Dickens had one of his characters in *The Old Curiosity Shop* voice a similar opinion from the punter's point of view: 'Would you care a ha'penny for the Lord Chancellor if you know'd him in private and without his wig? Certainly not.'

It seems the case for pantomimic fancy dress is clear. Not only does it identify the legal luminaries but it also lends dignity and formality to the grave business of the law itself.

Yet the case against is equally strong, for the paraphernalia of court dress isolates litigants from legal professionals, suggests a certain pomposity and imbues the law with mystical qualities beyond the grasp of the common man or woman.

Quite a conundrum, this wig business, which is why rather a stir was caused in 1992 when certain dissident voices within the profession suggested they be cast aside as part of a sweeping modernisation of the legal system. There was even talk of name badges for court officials, not to mention piped music and potted plants in the waiting areas. Where would it all end? 'Would the accused care for a massage before he enters the dock?'

It was all put to the test in November 1992 when a survey conducted by the Criminal Bar Association found that a resounding 72 per cent of its members were in favour of retaining their wigs for crown court cases.

The traditionalists rejoiced, none more so than Judge Hugh Jones, a county court judge since 1988 who took pride in his rather 'distressed' hairpiece. But on 10 November at Cardiff County Court it was Judge Jones who was distressed as the unthinkable happened. *The Times* gravely reported the heinous crime: 'A thief sneaked into the chambers of Judge Hugh Jones and stole his horsehair wig valued at £500, along with its box.'

Court officials were said to be hugely embarrassed by this supremely symbolic theft and a lawyer said, 'To say the judge was displeased is an understatement. A well-used wig shows authority and experience, so it's no good just going out to get a new one.'

Judge Jones was not available for comment and the culprit remained undetected.

This unsavoury but perversely delicious incident did nothing to stem the wig debate as those for and against continued to address the prickly subject from time to time. But as the century came to a close the lower echelons of the legal hierarchy were still sticking to their guns, insisting on donning the horsehair even though the Law Lords, the highest authority in the land, had long since ceased to do so.

Judicial rugs continued to make the news stories, including that under the deliciously intriguing headline RECORDER'S WIG FOUND IN ELECTRIC KETTLE, but perhaps the last word on the absurdity of the debate should go to one of the wiggy fraternity themselves.

In a letter to *The Times* of 2 February 1999 Lord Millett mused somewhat quizzically: 'English judges are an eccentric lot. When I had a full head of hair I wore a wig. Now I have no hair, I have dispensed with my wig.'

Judge Hugh Jones might have smiled at that. But probably not.

CAUGHT IN THE ACT

GREAT YARMOUTH MAGISTRATES' COURT, 1992

Some of the strangest cases in legal history are fictional, for on the written page or in film liberties can be taken that no court of law could possibly countenance:

> 'Give your evidence,' said the King, 'and don't be nervous, or I'll have you executed on the spot.'

It could surely only happen in Lewis Carroll's *Alice's Adventures in Wonderland* (1865). And would Spike Milligan really have dared to utter in court his delicious 1972 line from *The Last Goon Show of All*: 'Policemen are only numbered in case they get lost'?

Even in *The Law's Strangest Cases* those two would have difficulty passing muster as the authentic article, but in Norfolk on 9 July 1992 the lines of delineation between fact and fiction did become rather blurred. The result was that a habitual burglar serving two years at Norwich jail stood wrongfully accused of committing a crime that even he found too shameful to contemplate.

The prelude to Norman Douglass's unthinkably foul act was the 1989 survey by Norfolk Police that revealed that the costs of transporting remand prisoners from Norwich jail to Great Yarmouth Magistrates' Court were becoming prohibitive:

'The equivalent of 28 police officers are engaged full-time in escort duties each day,' said Inspector Phil Jones from his eerily deserted office. Might it be an idea, posed the powers that be, to introduce a live audio-visual link between the prison and the court? That way the prisoners could 'appear in court' without leaving jail. Inspector Jones had apparently seen the system used to great effect in Dade County, Florida, and in Toronto. Rudimentary Skype in all but name.

It was decided to run a four-week pilot scheme and four convicted prisoners at Norwich jail were press-ganged into adopting the roles of criminals. Little rehearsal was needed, although a couple of the prisoners did complain they might become typecast.

First up was Eben Gordon, in his twelfth year of a life sentence, asked to play the role of a juvenile burglar: 'You are Dan Shifty?' the prisoner was asked, showing his best side to the cameras as magistrates, a court clerk and two solicitors back in court in Great Yarmouth got into the swing of things amid all the paraphernalia of a real trial.

Shifty's sentence remains unrecorded although his alter ego Gordon did wish the court to know his feelings: 'Many remand prisoners like to travel from prison to court and back,' he pleaded. 'It's a day out, a break from prison routine.'

Next in the virtual dock was Jack Thumper, accused, you may not be amazed to learn, of serious assault. He was followed by Fred Biggs whose surname strangely belies the fact that he was actually charged with reckless driving. One would have imagined train robbery at the very least, bearing in mind the brilliant ingenuity of the prison scriptwriters.

Again the sentences of these two desperadoes remain unrecorded. That just left Norman Douglass, serving two years for burglary. I have no idea what poor Mr Douglass had done to upset the prison authorities but being asked to look straight into the camera in front of all his live-studio-audience colleagues to confirm that he was indeed 'Dick

Rumpole, an alcoholic shoplifter' didn't seem altogether fair.

But it wasn't that which really upset the hapless Norman, as he told a reporter from *The Times* sent to review his performance: 'The name and the drink problem didn't really worry me. What I find really embarrassing is the crime. I've been accused of stealing knickers from Marks and Spencer.'

Thus suitably shamed, Dick Rumpole, the depraved monster of the East Anglian under(wear)world, provided an instant answer to all those who seek to bring in stronger sentences or reintroduce the death penalty.

Forget it. Make 'em play charades or walk around the prison corridors dressed as Andy Pandy. A good dose of squirming embarrassment could yet be the solution reformers have spent centuries looking for.

A COMEDY OF ERRORS
LEWES CROWN COURT, 1998

No aspect of the law ought really to be a laughing matter, but the records show time and again that many court cases have a humorous side. All too often, however, that moment is a fleeting one and a swift reminder from the judge that 'this is no place for levity' is generally sufficient to restore a suitably sombre atmosphere in which the serious business of the courts can proceed.

Thank goodness, then, for the historic first at Lewes Crown Court on 4 September 1998, when a judge decided to halt a trial and declare the prisoner innocent because the entire court, including the police prosecution, was helpless with laughter.

Impersonating a police officer is a potentially serious crime. When the offence is coupled with damaging and stealing police property it's even worse. Breaking in to do the deed doesn't help the cause, and when the entire act is perpetrated at a police station itself, then it has to be said that the prospects for the offender don't look good.

But that was precisely the scenario facing 29-year-old Simon Davey after a night out that took a surprising turn.

The jury looked on with suitably intense concentration as Davey's story began. He had been to the Eastbourne Darts Open and, as darts spectators are wont to do, had got into the spirit of things with a spot of drinking: 'eight or ten pints', according to his evidence.

Having sensibly decided to have a taxi home, he realised halfway through the journey that he hadn't got any money to pay the fare. After alerting the driver to the impecunious state of his affairs, he was understandably turfed out without due ceremony.

It was probably the fresh air that then caused the effects of the beer to kick in. It seems that a well-meaning but equally half-baked logic and sense of fair play began to drive Davey's brain cells. What he obviously needed to do, he told himself, was report himself to the police so that they wouldn't pursue him for his terrible crime when the taxi driver spilt the beans.

In consequence of that honourable train of thought he dutifully made his way to Hailsham Police Station, East Sussex, in the dead of night to make his confession, but on his arrival there the station was locked and there was no one around. Again the solution was obvious – he would break in and leave his confession on an answering machine.

Now it has to be said at this stage that Simon Davey had a nice turn of phrase and a jaunty laddishness in his demeanour that made him rather a likeable soul, and if he'd been a professional comedian his catchphrase would certainly have been 'It's the way I tell 'em.'

Members of the jury began to smirk. They knew they shouldn't but they did and, rather like the taboo of getting the giggles in church, this only made matters worse. Shoulders began to move up and down, noses were blown, eye contact was avoided and cheeks were sucked in as Davey's yarn proceeded.

After he had climbed into the deserted station through a toilet window, they heard, his noble effort to leave a message failed dismally when he broke the machine. It was then that he saw the inspector's hat and sergeant's jacket hanging on a peg. Overcome by a sense of indignation that there was no one on the enquiry desk he donned the uniform and remedied the situation by manning the front office himself.

'And why did you do that?' asked the prosecution: 'Just in case there was another idiot like me that night. Someone needed to be on duty,' was the matter-of-fact reply. For good measure he went on to describe how he had then started filling out a statement form which he had found in a desk.

Bottoms shuffled uneasily in the jury box. Lips began to twitch uncontrollably. At least one handkerchief was now stuffed permanently into its owner's mouth and several jurors appeared to be in severe danger of wetting themselves as the story progressed.

When a passing special constable knocked on the door of the station in the early hours he was let in by Davey who, anxious to appear as authentic a policeman as possible, rocked back on his heels, flexed his knees and greeted the visitor with a cheery 'Evenin', all.'

The masquerade was unlikely to fool even a bobby of the hobby variety and reinforcements soon arrived. It was then that the taped interview was made, and Davey's explanation while he was still under the influence of eight to ten pints (did he spill the ninth or what?) was always going to make for interesting listening.

It was when the police prosecution insisted on playing the tape in court that all the laughter-stifling techniques of the jury and court officials finally gave way. As the court heard the hilarious story of Davey's night out 'as it happened' the corpsing of the jury began in earnest, quickly spreading to the lawyers and even the police officers present.

For the first time in its illustrious history *The Times* was moved to report: 'Judge Richard Brown had to stifle a chuckle as jurors wiped away tears.' It was then that Judge Richard Brown attained the state of mind that few judges before or since have managed to emulate – he saw the funny side. Ordering the tape to be stopped with Davey still in mid-babble he consulted lawyers for the defence and prosecution and duly directed the jury to deliver a verdict of not guilty.

They say laughter is the best medicine and it was certainly a tonic for Simon Davey as he walked free from court bound over to keep the peace for two years.

One man who would certainly have appreciated that uplifting end was a solicitor's clerk, Stephen Balogh, because his own attempts to lighten up court proceedings in 1974 ended in a jail sentence. When caught lurking on the roof of St Albans Crown Court he explained to police that he intended to release laughing gas into the ventilation system 'to liven up long-winded and boring court proceedings'.

That he failed in his mission was evidenced by the stern face of Mr Justice Melford Stevenson as he gave him six months. Nor was Balogh amused – as he left the mirth-free zone of Stevenson's court he shouted, 'You are a humourless automaton.'

SILENCE IN COURT
WINCHESTER CROWN COURT, 1999

JUDGE DELAYS TRIAL IN FAVOUR OF COURT, said *The Times*'s headline of 29 June 1999. That curious eye-catcher was echoed in every domestic newspaper in some form or another on the same day. The tabloids, in particular, had great fun at the expense of Judge Patrick Hooton, the unfortunate gentleman concerned. But he'd have been perfectly all right if only he'd kept his mouth shut. The trial of David Hunter, from Basildon, Essex, charged with indecent assault, was estimated to last four days. It was routine fare for 47-year-old Judge Hooton, called to the Bar in 1973 and a circuit judge since 1994. Nothing suggested the trial would become front-page news.

Proceedings were due to commence at Winchester Crown Court at midday on Monday, 28 June, but, as a start was made, the prosecution and defence told the judge that they'd probably need five or six days to see the trial through.

Judge Hooton's heart sank, for he knew he had a prior engagement on the Friday and was then off on holiday for four weeks after that. Being a diligent sort of fellow keen to see that the course of justice was properly run, he was concerned that the case might have to be rushed, so he made up his mind to ask the parties for an adjournment there and then. That was by no means a strange occurrence. It happens all the time.

He duly addressed the assembled lawyers: 'Unless I can

send the jury out first thing on Thursday morning I can't start this trial. It would not be right to make everyone feel they have got to rush it.'

Lawyers acting on the case saw no problem and the trial was put back for six months until December. If only Judge Hooton had left it there – but no, he'd pulled off something of a coup that year and just couldn't contain himself. He had to tell someone his wonderful news. Thus he proceeded:

'Some months ago I arranged to take this Friday off. I won't be doing anything this Friday apart from sitting at Wimbledon watching the tennis. Normally I would take the time for this case out of my holiday. Everybody knows my devotion to my duty but it's the tickets to Wimbledon, you see. I'm never likely to get them again.'

Robert Conway, agreeing to the adjournment for the defence, understood completely: 'Wimbledon is on my doorstep,' he lamented ruefully, 'but 1 can't get tickets.'

Judge Hooton replied with a smile: 'They are only given to the deserving.'

With that pleasant exchange the affair should have ended but the local press were present and made the most of their scoop. Soon the story of the judge who put the prospect of a men's semifinal before a case of indecent assault was national news: JUDGE POSTPONES ASSAULT TRIAL TO WATCH WIMBLEDON, bawled the *Guardian*.

Either you'll feel sorry for Judge Hooton or you won't. So often seen as aloof, placed on a pedestal of their own making, judges are, after all, human. Why shouldn't they enjoy themselves? But they are also well paid and have a responsibility to society. Shouldn't Patrick Hooton have missed the tennis for the sake of justice?

The camps will inevitably remain split, but what is certain is that Judge Hooton wasn't the first to let his passion for sport creep into courtroom proceedings. At the end of the nineteenth century there was always silence in court on at least one day a year when Mr Justice Hawkins was presiding. He routinely closed his court on Derby Day and that was that, even if the press did lambast him for it.

And during an important criminal trial in 1977 Judge Alan King-Hamilton famously interrupted proceedings to tell the jury, 'The Australians are four for one wicket.'

Cricket made an even more bizarre unscheduled appearance at a tax fraud trial in 1986. On that occasion Judge Michael Argyle opted to shoot himself in both feet by solemnly telling the jury that the lack of Test Match cricket on television was 'enough to make an Orthodox Jew want to join the Nazi party'. Eloquent and learned as they can be, perhaps all judges should know the predatory nature of the press well enough to take a leaf from the book of Mr Justice Cassels, one of the twentieth century's most characterful judges. As an aid to making his court a personal gaffe-free zone he invariably placed a large notice in front of himself on the bench, stating in capital letters: KEEP YOUR TRAP SHUT.

TRUST ME, I'M A DOCTOR
PRESTON CROWN COURT, 1999

It isn't everybody who gets into *The Law's Strangest Cases*. Some of the most evil and sensational murderers in history failed to get beyond the first selection stage simply because murder in itself just isn't an unusual enough occurrence to qualify as of right.

So Jack the Ripper (1888) failed to make the cut, as did the Boston Strangler (1964), the Black Panther (1976) and the bodies-in-the-drains murderer Dennis Nilsen (1983). The chillingly cool schoolgirl killer Mary Flora Bell (1968) also missed out, as did the two juvenile killers of two-year-old Jamie Bulger, whose inconceivable act of cruelty caused such outrage in 1993 and beyond. Even the Moors Murderers Myra Hindley and Ian Brady, given life sentences at Chester Assizes in 1966, scored insufficient points on the 'strangeometer' and they were joined by the Yorkshire Ripper Peter Sutcliffe (1981), the 25 Cromwell Street fiends Rose and Fred West (1994), and sundry other celebrity killers from several centuries of material.

That such a gruesome bunch should be upstaged by a mild-mannered, 54-year-old bespectacled doctor from the quiet town of Hyde in Cheshire might seem unlikely. But then there was a fair bit that was unlikely about Dr Harold Shipman, whose calculated dispatch of his patients to the other world gives him the title of Britain's worst ever serial killer.

Yet Shipman's catalogue of death might never have been uncovered but for the watchful tenacity of solicitor Angela Woodruff. When her 81-year-old mother, Kathleen Grundy, died in June 1998 Mrs Woodruff was naturally surprised to find that the bulk of her mother's substantial estate had been left to Harold Shipman, the doctor who had cared for her so ably and been there for her even at the moment of death. It was Mrs Woodruff's own detective work that exposed the will as a forgery, and it was her instinctive feeling that something more was amiss that then led her to persuade police to exhume her mother's body.

When they discovered it contained a lethal dose of morphine, suspicion fell instantly, but incredulously, on Shipman. But when police showed that it was certainly the good doctor who had forged the will, the case against him mounted and they began to investigate other deaths among his patients.

What they discovered horrified the residents of Hyde, for it became apparent that Shipman, under the guise of showing the utmost professional concern, had taken to visiting his women patients in their homes. There, in a firm but gentle tone that his ailing ladies heard as 'Trust me, I'm a doctor', Shipman would suggest an injection to relieve their symptoms. And relieve them it did, for there they would die of the lethal morphine dose as Shipman informed the relatives that he had done 'everything possible' to preserve their lives.

As the case received huge media coverage, more and more relatives came forward to police expressing retrospective concern over the circumstances in which their loved ones had died. Soon the confirmed tally of suspicious deaths had reached the horrifying count of 15 and Shipman was eventually tried on that indictment at Preston Crown Court in October 1999.

But 15 proved merely to be a fraction of the true count as more and more bodies were exhumed and coroners found lethal doses of morphine time and again in both male and female victims. By the time the trial began, experts suggested that over a hundred deaths might be laid at Shipman's door, spanning his entire medical career.

Such revelations undoubtedly didn't help his cause, but during the 57-day trial Shipman stared impassively in court and protested his innocence throughout. His wife Primrose, married to him for 33 years and mother of their four children, was present in court every day to support her beloved husband. When the trial closed, the jury deliberated for 34 hours and the foreman took six minutes to deliver the verdict. Dr Harold Shipman, the man with the worst bedside manner in history, was duly found unanimously guilty of murdering 15 women between the ages of 49 and 81. On Wednesday, 2 February 2000, he was convicted and given 15 terms of life imprisonment.

Mr Justice Forbes articulated the horror of a nation as he passed sentence: 'I have little doubt each of your victims smiled and thanked you as she submitted to your deadly administrations. None of these ladies realised that yours was not a healing touch.'

The South Manchester Coroner, meanwhile, compounded that horror by confirming that Shipman's likely tally had reached 265 and suggesting that 'the final figure might prove to be as high as a thousand'. The true figure will never be fully ascertained but Harold Shipman proved to a Britain entering the enlightened twenty-first century that deeds more suited to the most far-fetched Victorian melodrama can still be perpetrated in our very midst.

Could anyone possibly dispute that the man they called 'Doctor Death' and 'The Dr Jekyll of Hyde' deserves his place in *The Law's Strangest Cases*? It is unlikely Britain will ever see his like again – but then that has been said before.

THE SCALES OF JUSTICE
SUNDERLAND MAGISTRATES' COURT,
2000

The connection between the philosophical concept of 'Justice' and the physical act of 'weighing' is as old as civilisation itself. In ancient Egyptian mythology the god Osiris presided in the Hall of Two Truths, where the souls of the dead were weighed in the balance against a feather of truth, which symbolised the just treatment of one's fellow men – those wretched souls who failed the balance test were devoured forthwith by a fearsome monster.

It is the same principle that lies behind the world-famous statue of the goddess Justitia, which stands on the summit of the Old Bailey, holding in her left hand the scales of justice and in her right the double-edged sword to punish the guilty.

All of which symbolic talk is particularly pertinent to the case that follows because many things were weighed in the balance along the way. *Thoburn v. Sunderland City Council* was dubbed variously as 'Britain v. Europe', 'David v. Goliath' and 'Common Sense v. Gobbledegook' – it earned a 36-year-old greengrocer, Steve Thoburn, the tag of 'Metric Martyr' and put his picture in all the leading newspapers. Steve Thoburn had handled many cases of bananas in his life but never one quite like this.

The date of 1 January 2000 may have been heralded as the start of a new millennium but it was the start of an altogether new era for Britain's greengrocers as a European directive decreed that they must sell all their loose produce using either solely metric scales or ones that had both metric and imperial measures. Such a directive from the European Economic Community was a not entirely unexpected consequence of Britain's willingly joining the Common Market in 1972 and it was issued as a phased control pending full metrication in 2009.

Suffice to say, though, that the person in the street was by and large not impressed and many of the nation's greengrocers ignored the directive and happily continued to weigh and sell a pound of whatever they fancied – it was, they insisted, what their customers preferred.

It was only a matter of time before someone took this weighty issue entirely at face value and in July 2000 it was the trading standards officers of Sunderland City Council who decided to prosecute in what was destined to become a test case of national interest.

Steve Thoburn was the hapless victim as Lynda Hodgson, undercover trading standards officer, went to his shop and bought a bunch of bananas for 34 pence. They were priced at 25 pence a pound and Mr Thoburn weighed them in pounds and ounces on scales not delineated in metric.

Steve Thoburn was duly prosecuted under the Weights and Measures Act 1985, an action that immediately sparked off a silly season for quotes and punny headlines: Vivian Linacre of the British Weights and Measures Society suggested that 'maybe the Brussels bureaucrats would like to change my name to Vivian Linhectare' while fishmonger Neil Herron threw his support firmly behind his greengrocer chum with the splendid, 'If Prime Minister Blair's baby Leo can weigh in at 6 pounds, 12 ounces, then it's good enough for a haddock.' Others asked why the McDonald's burger chain were allowed to sell their famous Quarter Pounders and daftness surely reached new heights when a pensioner, Ernest Riley, phoned his local radio station trying to start a campaign to rid Brussels sprouts of the evil 'B' word:

'They look like small cabbages,' he said, 'so we ought to call them 'minicabs'. Sorry, Ernest, next caller, please. By the time the preliminary hearing was due to start at Sunderland Magistrates' Court on 15 January 2001 Steve Thoburn had already been dubbed the 'Metric Martyr' and huge numbers of Britain's Euro-sceptics, Ernest included, prepared for battle.

A fine of up to £2,000 or a jail sentence if he refused to pay lay in wait for Steve Thoburn, but it was the principle of British Law v. European Law that became the much bigger issue. With so much at stake a decision was delayed until Monday, 9 April 2001, when the eyes of a nation again turned to Sunderland Magistrates' Court as District Judge Bruce Morgan announced the long-awaited verdict:

'This case revolves around possibly the most famous bunch of bananas in legal history,' he told a packed court. His mystifying use of the word 'possibly' seemed a mite superfluous as he continued by finding the 'Metric Martyr' guilty and ordering for his illegal scales to be destroyed.

At a stroke a judge in an English court of law had overtly confirmed that European Union directives must take precedence over the laws of the British Parliament!

Steve Thoburn escaped with a conditional discharge but he was still accorded hero status by much of the British press for his stand. *The Daily Mail* headline screamed THE DAY SELLING A POUND OF BANANAS BECAME A CRIME LIKE BURGLARY OR RAPE, while trading standards officers all over Britain prepared to pay their 'friendly local greengrocer' a surprise visit.

Where will it all end? ask the sceptics. Everything seemed headed for an inevitable victory for Europe.

While Steve Thoburn contemplated an appeal, ardent traditionalists urged more direct action. One newspaper correspondent said: 'He should employ a steeplejack to scale the Old Bailey and place a giant bunch of bananas in Justitia's scales complete with '25p a lb' price tag and a notice on her thrusting sword saying UP THE EUROPEAN UNION.'

It might not have killed the kilo but what more fruitful way of marking the day the law went bananas?

CALL BRENDAN MICHAEL FORRESTER

DERBY MAGISTRATES' COURT, 2001

When Crown Prosecution solicitor Ian Shaw arrived at Derby Magistrates' Court on Tuesday, 6 March 2001, there was one listed case that took him by surprise because Derbyshire Police had not sent him the case file.

That in itself was by no means a unique occurrence and he hoped for a quick briefing to bring him up to press so that the prosecution on behalf of the force could proceed as if nothing untoward had happened.

But what did happen next *was* a unique occurrence, and it left Derbyshire Police and court staff with very eggy faces and Ian Shaw furious that his time had been wasted.

When he looked at the computer-generated list of cases that morning the list of charges against Brendan Michael Forrester astonished him. Perhaps it was no wonder the file was missing, for such would have been its thickness that a special freight delivery would surely have been needed.

The computer records showed that 28-year-old Forrester, of Kingsway Place, Swadlincote, was charged with 11 offences on 4 January – and what reading they made: six motoring offences including death by dangerous driving, two drugs charges, obstructing a police officer, possessing a rocket launcher and living off immoral earnings.

Ian Shaw was taken aback: 'He must be one of Derbyshire's most wanted men. Looking at this list of charges it's amazing that a person like this would ever have been granted bail.'

As Shaw girded his loins to prosecute as well as he could without full notes he prepared himself for coming face to face with this evident desperado, but when court staff called Brendan Michael Forrester he was nowhere to be found. Several hours passed and still he failed to turn up.

Court officials became concerned. Should a man with his record really be at large? The rocket launcher sounded particularly ominous. Surely he was a danger to the good people of Derbyshire.

By lunchtime Forrester was still missing and Crown Prosecution Service representatives called Derbyshire Police to establish his possible whereabouts.

Did you ever see the magnificently incompetent Will Hay as Sergeant Dudfoot, ably hindered by Albert and Harbottle, in the 1939 film *Ask a Policeman*! It would be difficult to imagine more farcical antics ever being repeated on celluloid, let alone in real life. But maybe they should have made the sequel, *Ask a Derbyshire Policeman*, which would have taken comedy genius to new heights.

Having looked into this most disturbing matter, a police representative telephoned the Magistrates' Court with his findings: 'We have no record of a fatal road accident on 4 January,' he said, 'nor do we have a record of an arrest of Brendan Michael Forrester.'

It got worse: 'He doesn't appear on the electoral register either, and there is no such address as Kingsway Court, Swadlincote.'

Again it got worse: 'What I'm saying to you is that Brendan Michael Forrester doesn't actually exist. Except on the computer. That's why he's on your court list.'

Initial relief at court that such a supposedly dangerous man wasn't actually on the loose soon gave way to embarrassment and anger amid much finger-pointing. 'The police log the cases on to the system,' claimed court officials. 'But not all of them,' countered the force. 'Some of your people have direct access.'

Ian Shaw was not amused. Turning up to prosecute phantoms wasn't his line. The deputy justices clerk Margaret Shanahan was left to face the press, already sharpening their pencils gleefully: 'It appears we have a fictional case on our hands,' she explained. 'A full investigation has been launched.'

As Ian Shaw left the court in a furious temper he gave his own take on this curious affair: 'I'll push for someone to get to the bottom of this. It looks very much like a police training exercise that went too far.'

In the event Derbyshire Police were let off the hook as it emerged that a 23-year-old employee of the Magistrates' Court had created the mystery criminal for a spot of fun during his lunch break. He was charged under the Computer Misuse Act 1990.

It must have been a great relief to the people of Derbyshire to be assured that their police force were not the buffoons that this unique case at first suggested.

Rumours that 'The Phantom' remained at large, and that a certain Miss Marple had been put on the case, were dismissed as 'entirely fictional.'

A CHANCY CONVICTION
COURT OF APPEAL, LONDON, 2003

Two centuries ago a mischievous lawyer classified 'unreliable witnesses' into 'simple liars, damned liars, and experts.' That spawned the celebrated variation 'there are lies, damned lies, and statistics'. Together the aphorisms suggest a lethal cocktail – an expert witness armed with statistics. Witness the initial verdict in the great miscarriage of justice *The Crown v. Sally Clark* (1999).

After Clark was found guilty of double murder, disquieted voices asserted she had been 'convicted by statistics'. Only in the Court of Appeal on 29 January 2003 were the convictions overturned – by then Clark had served the three years inside, which hastened her tragic end.

On 9 November 1999, then a 35-year-old mother of one, Sally Clark had been convicted at Chester Crown Court of the murder of her first two children. Her first, Christopher, had died three years earlier aged 11 weeks, the death initially ascribed to natural causes from 'Sudden Infant Death Syndrome' (SIDS) commonly labelled 'cot death'.

Her second, Harry, died aged eight weeks just over a year later. After declaring this death 'suspicious', the Home Office revisited Christopher's case and determined that suspicious too. Sally Clark was arrested and committed to trial. By profession a solicitor, also married to one, and the daughter of a senior police officer, she expressed profound respect for the law and declared her innocence.

Nine medical specialists failed to prove that Clark was a killer. Experts for the defence declared the cause of both deaths 'unclear'. The prosecution then called expert witness Professor Sir Roy Meadow, a highly-respected authority in child abuse. But not a highly-respected statistician.

Yet Meadow's forceful proposal that neither child had died a natural death was backed by a host of impressive-sounding figures. He had strayed from his field of expertise into the minefield of probability theory.

Such evidence ought to have been inadmissible – Meadow had no expertise in numbers. But neither did the judge, defence team or jury – that sealed Sally Clark's fate. Bamboozled by the stats – perhaps embarrassed by their own shortcomings – no one in court questioned the Professor's number juggling. Heads were nodded sagely, chins stroked and glazing eyes turned aloft. Strangest of all, the defence failed to call a statistical expert to demolish the Professor's figures. Had they done so, Sally Clark may have walked free at the initial trial.

The Professor presented his numbers with apparent unequivocal logic: 'The risk of a single child of that age and background dying of SIDS is 1 in 8,543 live births. To calculate the same fate befalling two children from the same family we simply have to multiply 1 in 8,543 by itself. This gives a chance of approximately 1 in 73 million that two such natural SIDS deaths would occur. Put another way, taking total population into account, these double 'cot deaths' would only occur by chance once every 100 years. Therefore an unnatural cause of death, namely murder, very strongly suggests itself.'

A little knowledge is a dangerous thing. It was for Sally Clark. By using the 'probability multiplier' method Professor Meadow had made a fundamental error. That calculation holds only if the two 'events' (deaths) are entirely independent of each other with no risk of 'connection' – like rolling the same number with a single die twice running.

Meadow had failed to adjust his figures for genetic or hereditary propensity, and other causal links. Had he done so, his persuasive 1 in 73 million figure would have been dramatically reduced. A later article in the *British Medical Journal* suggested that once one SIDS death had occurred, a second in the same family might occur in England once every 18 months – rather different to Meadow's '100 years'.

Meadow had strayed dangerously close to 'schoolboy howler' territory. In addition he perpetrated the 'Prosecutor's Fallacy' – establishing that an innocent explanation is so highly improbable that a guilty one must be probable in precisely the same ratio. Revisiting the 1 in 73 million chance that both infants died naturally, Meadow asserted that the chance of Sally Clark NOT being a double murderer must be the same. Things didn't look good for Clark.

But again Meadow had over-simplified and ignored external factors. The fallacy of logic comes to mind – 'All cats have four legs. My dog has four legs. Therefore my dog is a cat.' Yet the jury were not to know they were being duped. Nor was Professor Meadow yet finished. Having delivered his 'likelihood of natural death' figures he framed the argument in popular terms as 'like backing an 80 to 1 winning outsider in the Grand National four years running'. A tasteless comparison given the tragic circumstances of the case, but one the jury understood. Had any of them backed even a single winner in The National? Probably not … ergo the deaths *must* have been deliberate.

Summing up, Mr Justice Harrison sounded a note of caution: 'We do not convict people in these courts on statistics. It would be a terrible day if that were so.' It was a terrible day for Sally Clark – in the glare of national publicity she was convicted of double murder by a 10–2 majority, receiving two life sentences.

After her first appeal was dismissed on 2 October 2000, it was discovered that medical evidence, which might have provided an innocent explanation for Harry's death, had not been disclosed to the defence. That changed everything. Her second appeal was allowed in 2003 and she was set free. Even so, the main ground for acquittal was 'new medical evidence' rather than 'flawed statistics'.

But it was too late for Sally Clark. Her law-related background ensured she suffered a torrid time inside. Psychologically broken, she died unintentionally aged 42 on 16 March 2007 due to 'acute alcohol intoxication.'

It is impossible to prove how much the jury was swayed by Professor Meadow's creative figures, but statisticians later took up Sally Clark's cause with a vengeance. The Royal Statistical Society introduced initiatives to better equip legal professionals to understand numerical complexities, particularly targeting graduates whose 'grasp of figures is often sorely wanting.'

As for Roy Meadow, the General Medical Council struck him from the British Medical Register. This was later overturned on appeal, but following fierce criticism Meadow relinquished his registration voluntarily in 2009.

The strangest element in *The Crown v. Sally Clark* is that Clark was ever found guilty at all – proof that numbers can be powerful tools, and that the curiosities of statistics are a closed book to many outside the discipline. Writing in 2009 Vincent Scheurer – expert in 'statistics and the law' – summed up: 'What is striking is that, within a sea of complexity, the staggering figure of 1 in 73 million stands out like a beacon of simplicity. Unfortunately for Sally Clark, far from being a lighthouse to the truth, this figure was both irrelevant and wrong.'

There is scarcely room for levity in such a tragic case. But the odds are heavily against me not giving the last word to an anonymous wag with a keen eye for figures: 'Let's face it, 98 per cent of people know full well that 92.5 per cent of all statistics are completely made up. And that's 100 per cent fact.'

IN GOD WE TRUST
TIMISOARA, ROMANIA, 2005

In Washington DC on 30 July 1956 a law passed by the Eighty-fourth Congress – approved by President Eisenhower – formally declared 'In God We Trust' the national motto of the United States of America. A year later it was added to America's paper currency – having first appeared on its coins in 1864.

Although not implying national observance of one religion, the phrase clearly encapsulates a fundamental tenet of the Christian faith. Those who place themselves in God's hands will be shown the 'right path' in life.

That comforting message, incorporated into countless hymns and patriotic songs, also resonates in biblical verses. Psalm 32:8 is particularly alluring: 'I will instruct thee and teach thee in the way which thou shalt go.' While Proverbs 29:25 suggests a cast-iron insurance policy: 'Whoso putteth his trust in the Lord shall be safe.'

What's good for America can surely serve Romania. There Pavel Mircea – baptised in childhood – was confident his life's journey with God as guide would be a guaranteed success. But he took a wrong turn and was convicted of murder.

Mircea professed himself sorely betrayed, and in 2005 the 40-year-old prisoner pursued the ultimate redress. Seeking self-absolution as much as financial gain, he attempted to sue God for breach of contract.

The submission to Timisoara Court of Justice in western Romania made it clear who he blamed: 'I the undersigned Pavel M, currently jailed at Timisoara serving 20 years for murder, request legal action against God, resident in Heaven, and represented here by the Romanian Orthodox Church, for committing the following crimes; fraud, breach of trust, abuse of a position of authority, and misappropriation of goods.'

The inmate argued that his baptism was a contract between him and God, and that God had reneged on the deal: 'He was supposed to protect me from all evil, but instead gave me to Satan, who encouraged me to kill. God even accepted offerings and prayers from me, in exchange for forgiveness and the promise that I would be rid of problems and have a better life. But on the contrary I was left in the Devil's hands.'

Superficially this appeared a frivolous litigation – but it presented a conundrum, which needed careful handling. Rejecting the case on grounds that 'there is no proof God exists' was scarcely a feasible option – religious faith is strong in Romania. And God after all is recognised by legal authority. Witnesses in UK courts 'swear by Almighty God' on oath – in America 'so help me God' serves a similar purpose. And 'Acts of God' loom large in countless disputed insurance cases. So if advanced legal systems acknowledge God's existence, why should He not be sued by a disgruntled Romanian prisoner?

This innovative lawsuit took two years to resolve. In July 2007 the public prosecutor's office in Timisoara finally rejected the case on the grounds that God is not a person 'in the eyes of the law' and more particularly 'has no legal address at which the necessary papers can be served.'

Having lost his case Pavel Mircea was condemned to accept responsibility for his murderous past. Constantin Stoica, spokesman for the Romanian Orthodox Church in Bucharest, told reporters: 'The prison chaplain has the difficult task of explaining to him that God does not act without our will, and that people have the freedom to choose between good and evil.'

That might have been the end of the 'Man v. God' saga – but the case appeared quickly to inspire another. In America 71-year-old Nebraska State Senator Ernie Chambers already had a maverick reputation when on 14 September 2007 – just two months after Mircea's dismissal – he filed his own lawsuit against God. He declared it 'a mischievous protest intended to highlight the vast numbers of frivolous litigants increasingly wasting the courts' time.'

Chambers sought a permanent injunction ordering God to stop causing 'widespread death, destruction and terrorisation of millions of the Earth's inhabitants.' The suit further listed God's unconstrained wrath, including 'fearsome floods, horrendous hurricanes, earthquakes, plagues, famine, genocidal wars, birth defects, terrifying tornadoes and the like.'

Amidst much media interest this again presented a dilemma – for this was America … official motto 'In God We Trust'. But Marlon Polk, Douglas County district court judge, doggedly adopted the Romanian stance that God had no address at which to serve papers: 'Given that this court finds there can never be service effectuated on the named defendant, this action will be dismissed with prejudice.'

But Chambers countered with incisive logic: 'The court acknowledges the existence of God and by extension recognises God's omniscience. God is therefore present in Douglas County and knows everything. So God already has knowledge of this lawsuit.'

Chambers appealed the judge's decision. The semantic arguments might have lasted decades, but common sense blessedly prevailed. On 24 February 2009 Nebraska Court of Appeals dismissed Chambers' appeal and closed the case.

With that, the idea of 'suing God' appeared to wane. But

there have been parallel debates concerning other ethereal characters ... not least the legal standing of Santa Claus, whose existence like God's is sometimes questioned. This was memorably addressed in the film *Miracle on 34th Street* (1994) in which Kris Kringle (aka Santa Claus) was required by a New York court to prove himself 'the real one'. His defence produced as evidence a dollar bill and a compelling question: 'If the US Treasury embrace "In God We Trust", then why can't the people of New York believe in Santa Claus?' Mr Kringle won his case.

It goes without saying that Santa does exist. But the God debate is more complex. Who is to blame for the miseries of life? Perhaps the Bible should have the final word. Its verdict on God is naturally 'Not Guilty' – instead it casts grave aspersions on the perennial fall guys. Luke 11:46 – Jesus to a gathered throng – 'Woe to you lawyers ... for you load people with burdens hard to bear.'

THE MISSING PANTS
WASHINGTON DC, UNITED STATES, 2007

Let's start by making it clear. No one is without underwear here. In Britain we'd label this case 'The Wrong Trousers'. Blessedly the quirks of American-English add real value – headlines like 'JUDGE CRIES OVER MISSING PANTS' don't come along often enough. So we'll stick with 'pants'.

The trial in *Pearson v. Chung* – better known in America as the 'pants lawsuit' – began in the District of Columbia Superior Court on 12 June 2007. The civil action had initially been filed in 2005 by Judge Roy L. Pearson, but its seeds were sown in 2002 when Pearson – then a legal aid lawyer – took a pair of pants to his neighbourhood store Custom Dry Cleaners. When the pants were misplaced Pearson accepted modest compensation of $150 from South Korean proprietors Jin and Soo Chung.

The couple had emigrated in search of 'the American dream' but were headed for a nightmare. Although Pearson had apparently accepted his recompense – and continued to use Custom Dry Cleaners – a grudge began to fester.

Three years passed before 57-year-old Pearson landed a job as an administrative law judge. On 3 May 2005 – keen to look sharp in his first week – he took five expensive suits into Custom Dry Cleaners for alterations … his expanding waistline had rendered the pants uncomfortably tight. Four were returned on time but one pair of pants was initially misplaced and came back late. A furiously indignant

Pearson refused to accept them, claiming they were not his pants at all, this despite the tag matching his receipt.

Highlighting the store's 'Satisfaction Guaranteed' and 'Same Day Service' signs he demanded $1,150 as the price of replacing the pants. When the Chungs refused – insisting they were the right pants – Pearson decided to 'take the cleaners to the cleaners'.

The 'wrong pants' suddenly took a price hike – claiming damages for 'discomfort, inconvenience and mental anguish', and a spurious array of consequent costs calculated over his entire life expectancy, Judge Pearson came up with his figure ... a shade over $65 million.

Prior to trial the Chungs made three offers – $3,000, $4,000 and finally $12,000 – all rejected by Pearson as derisory. Only when Superior Court Judge Neil Kravitz stated that 'the court has significant concerns that the plaintiff is acting in bad faith' did Pearson soften his demands. On 30 May 2007 he reduced his claim from $65 million to a sum he considered quite reasonable – $54 million.

When the trial opened, the plaintiff now dubbed 'Judge Fancy Pants' conducted his own defence with full histrionics. Recounting the emotional pain of the day 'the cleaners tried to pass off a cheaper pair of pants as mine' Judge Pearson broke down in tears and requested a break. After recovering his composure he called his star witness – the 89-year-old woman in a wheelchair told the court: 'I was chased out of that cleaners by an angry owner – they behave like Nazis in there.'

Throughout proceedings Pearson presented himself as the victim of a huge malicious fraud – one that had global ramifications for all customers of dry cleaners. This prompted a stern rebuke from Judge Judith Bartnoff: 'You are not a we, you are an I. You are seeking damages on your own behalf, not for the entire world.' Pearson then said of the Chungs' evil doings: 'You will search the DC archives in vain for a more egregious or wilful conduct.'

In response the Chungs' lawyer portrayed Pearson as a bitter insolvent man, who under questioning admitted that at the start of the case his ruinous divorce settlement had left him with barely $2,000 in the bank. Meanwhile a heart-warming picture emerged of the Chungs – a decent honest couple who sought nothing more in life than to deliver the right pants to the people of America.

Even in *The Law's Strangest Cases* it would be 'complete pants' for Pearson to win this one. The trial ended on 25 June 2007 with Judge Bartnoff ruling for Custom Dry Cleaners. The 'wrong pants' had indeed been Pearson's – and the Chungs' advertising signage was not fraudulent since 'no reasonable person would consider it made an unconditional promise.'

There this classic of vexatious litigation – noted for the 'breathtaking magnitude of the damages sought' – ought to quietly end. But Judge Roy Pearson wouldn't let it lie. Not content with losing both his case and his pants – which remained unclaimed in the office of the Chungs' lawyer – he also lost his job and $100,000 salary. After unsuccessfully appealing the 'pants lawsuit' he was told in November 2007 that his appointment with the Office of Administrative Hearings would not be extended, not least because he had 'demonstrated a lack of judicial temperament' in the pants case.

But again Pearson wouldn't go quietly. This time he sued Washington DC for wrongful dismissal, claiming a mere $1 million and demanding his job back. He also pursued further redress in the pants case. Yet again he was rebuffed. But only in May 2010 – after Pearson missed a deadline to go all the way to the US Supreme Court – did the long-running dispute finally come to an end.

Although much lampooned for its comedic value, the case had some serious overtones. As a result the legal profession in America began to examine ways of reducing the numbers of frivolous cases coming to court. It was considered particularly damaging that 'one of their own' should have taken such a ridiculous case so far. And businesses were advised to attach watertight conditions to promises such as 'Satisfaction Guaranteed'.

Yet if only Judge Pearson hadn't put on that extra weight in middle-life, the entire sorry affair might have been avoided. But then strangeology would have been the loser – for the 'pants lawsuit' takes some beating.

Perhaps the only saving grace for Roy Pearson was that he didn't also entrust his 'waistcoat' and a pair of 'braces' to Custom Dry Cleaners. Then American-English might have given us its finest headline: 'JUDGE CRIES OVER LOST VEST, PANTS AND SUSPENDERS'. Perhaps another time … one can but hope.

A LABYRINTHINE CASE
THE HIGH COURT, LONDON, 2008

On the surface the High Court judgment in *Hackney Borough Council v. Lyttle* on 14 April 2008 seemed unremarkable. Seventy-seven-year-old retired civil engineer William Lyttle had allowed his detached Victorian home 121 Mortimer Road, Hackney – in a fashionable part of north-east London – to fall into such disrepair that Hackney Council judged it unsafe. Exhortations to effect repairs had gone unheeded. Pressurised by neighbour unrest the Council took action.

The High Court ordered Lyttle to pay the Council £283,026 for essential repairs, plus £10,000 legal costs. At first glance only the figures stood out – one of the highest ever awards in a public nuisance case.

But an appended injunction suggested hidden depths. Ordering Lyttle to keep away from the property the judge warned 'there is evidence that he will, if unrestrained, undo the work.' For by that time Lyttle had garnered national fame for his destructive habits – and the nickname 'Mole Man'.

Soon after inheriting the 20-roomed residence in the 1960s, Lyttle began what he called 'home improvements'. Yet externally the property gradually deteriorated to a decrepit shell, its plot strewn with rubble.

The conundrum began to unravel only in 2003 when concerned neighbours highlighted untoward happenings – in 2001 a pavement near the property had collapsed, yielding a gaping gash. Another time the street was plunged into darkness – 'someone' had cut through a 420 volt cable.

When Hackney Council investigated fully in 2006, the truth 'emerged' – which Lyttle himself did rarely. For almost 40 years he had been secretly tunnelling under his property from his basement using nothing more than a shovel and a home-made pulley mechanism to remove the spoil – around 100m^3 (3,500 cu. ft) of it. That's a lot of earth – the Council's survey revealed over 20 tunnels about 3ft (0.9m) wide radiating up to 32ft (9.8m) in all directions at up to 13ft (4m) deep. Lyttle had used some as a novel waste disposal system – secreted in their depths were the remnants of three Renault cars and a boat, along with several fridges and numerous televisions. Above ground too the house was stashed with junk – Lyttle was an inveterate hoarder.

After his subterranean antics were revealed, the 'Mole Man' tag quickly followed, and the shabbily-bearded Lyttle was thrust blinkingly and reluctantly into the media spotlight – by nature he preferred a low profile. Headline writers had great fun – 'THE ONLY WAY IS DOWN', 'HOLEY MOLEY!', 'THE JOY OF WRECKS' – and a cult 1950s pop song by The Southlanders enjoyed a spike in its play-time … 'I am a mole and I live in a hole'.

But to the key question, 'Why?' Lyttle perfected a line in mischievous deflection – 'I first tried to dig a wine cellar, then it doubled, and so on. I just have a big basement. Tunnelling should be talked about without panicking.'

Hackney Borough Council begged to differ. In August 2006 they obtained a court order to temporarily evict Lyttle in order to fill the tunnels with concrete. Council surveyor Phillip Wilman told Thames Magistrates' Court: 'There has been ground movement. He's fortunate a London bus isn't in his front garden.'

Lyttle might fittingly have 'gone down' but instead was put into a hotel, where he remained for three years at a cost to the Council of £45,000.

Following the 2008 High Court award Lyttle's debt continued to mount as repair costs escalated. He never returned home and was moved in 2009 to a Council flat – pointedly on the top floor of a tower-block. After he died there in 2010 the Council discovered one last surprise – unable to burrow, he had instead gone sideways, knocking a huge hole between rooms. This raised his final liability to £408,000, which the Council pursued from his estate.

Despite that costly legacy William Lyttle had become a cult figure to Hackney's most creative thinkers. Fearing its demolition, artists and photographers vied to capture 'Mole House' for posterity. A folk song celebrated Lyttle's life. And a mock Blue Plaque was unveiled – 'William 'Mole Man' Lyttle 1931–2010, burrower, lived and dug here.'

In July 2012 'Mole House' was sold for £1.12 million to the internationally-renowned radical-contemporary artists Sue Webster and Tim Noble. Although the site had planning permission for two new dwellings they opted for preservation: 'In honour of 'Mole Man' we aim to keep as much of the original as possible, and to trace the area of his tunnels to create a basement.' They also planned the ultimate tribute – a sunken garden.

So the spirit of 'Mole Man' survives. One who knew him well believed he deserved it: 'He was very intelligent and a total gentleman. Yes he could be difficult, but his cheerfulness and kindness will live long in the memory.'

As for motive, Lyttle departed leaving everyone in the dark: 'I don't mind the title of inventor. Inventing things that don't work is a brilliant thing. People ask what the big secret is. And you know what? There isn't one.'

A final burning question remains. Was William Lyttle cremated? Or given the eternal peace below ground he surely craved? As the enigmatic 'Mole Man' might have said – for the answer to that you'll need to do some more digging.

YOUTH v. EXPERIENCE
EXETER CROWN COURT, 2012

At Exeter Crown Court in February 2012 a 22-year-old air conditioning engineer David Boyes from Belper, Derbyshire, stood accused of dangerous driving. In July 2009 the keen amateur cricketer had been returning from a club tour to Dorset – detouring via Devon – when his Vauxhall Corsa veered across the road near Axminster and hit another Corsa driven by 24-year-old bank employee Sarah Farquhar. Her horrific injuries included two broken thighs, a broken leg, broken toes and a broken collar bone.

On Boyes' passenger seat police found an iPod stopped in mid-track and a mobile phone. The prosecution held Boyes was distracted by changing tracks or checking text messages. Things didn't look good for the young cricketer. To avoid being given 'out' he needed a very good excuse.

Whether it was 'good' or just highly 'creative' the jury had to decide. After pleading his case Boyes said: 'I am asking the jury to accept that something strange happened that had not happened before, and that there was nothing wrong with my driving.' The 'something strange' involved a vicious assailant unable to proffer evidence – an unidentified Weymouth wasp, which had stung Boyes on the leg. The attack had occurred about noon – the collision occurred some six hours later. Boyes tried to link the two events.

As a boy he had suffered an extreme allergic reaction to a wasp sting. That much was true. But to the recent sting there had been no initial reaction – after waiting until 4.30p.m. 'just to be safe', he left Weymouth to begin his drive home. Boyes claimed his crash was caused by a sudden total blackout due to a severe delayed reaction to the sting.

The jury might have been seduced. But doubts emerged concerning Boyes' honesty. Immediately after the crash he made no reference to the sting, instead saying he had swerved to avoid a deer. Only later was the wasp implicated. But who could prove that the sting hadn't indeed caused a reaction? Boyes fancied his chance of getting off.

But he had bargained without the voice of experience. The prosecution called expert witness Dr William Frankland. The eminent immunologist told the court: 'A delayed reaction can occur, but only if there has been an initial extreme reaction. In all my years I have never known such a delayed reaction in isolation. This would be a world medical first.'

This is an unusual case in itself. But its 'strange' status is sealed by the expert witness – in particular that phrase 'in all my years' – for Dr Frankland was just a few days short of his one hundredth birthday, thought to be the oldest expert witness ever to give evidence. Here was a man who 60 years previously had worked with the discoverer of penicillin Alexander Fleming – and against his word stood a young lad with an unlikely story … one he had already changed.

Seizing the opportunity prosecutor Emily Pitts addressed Boyes: 'You are asking the jury to accept you are a medical miracle rather than a liar.' The jury didn't believe in miracles. The 'Weymouth Wasp' was absolved from all blame and Boyes was sentenced to 14 months in prison. *The Times* said: 'FLEMING'S ASSISTANT STILL CARRIES A STING ON EVE OF HIS 100TH BIRTHDAY.'

Stinging creatures – more commonly bees – have figured in a surprising number of unusual legal cases. Typically the shock of a sudden sting is cited by desperate defendants as the cause of some 'involuntary' action like speeding or discharging a firearm. As such the poor innocent bee is much maligned.

But there is a more serious side to 'Bees and the Law' – indeed a number of publications have that very title. Largely they cover bees in private ownership – what are the liabilities and responsibilities of a bee-keeper? Can a neighbour kill a bee that 'trespasses' onto their land? Who owns a swarm if it leaves a hive?

In 1941 G.W. Paton, Professor of Jurisprudence at Melbourne University, Australia, mused: 'A bee's propensity to sting has led certain counsel to suggest that they should be classed as dangerous animals. But even the most enthusiastic apiarist could hardly be held to have actual or constructive knowledge of the habits of a particular bee.'

In April 2015 this was put to the test on the tiny Hawaiian island of Kauai. Luis Soltren – allergic to bee stings – had been stung by a bee which he said belonged to his policeman neighbour Jesse Castro. Soltren was rushed to hospital and recovered – but sued Castro for modest medical expenses. Soltren told the court: 'To me there is no difference between a bullet and a bee – both could kill me.' Beekeeper Castro insisted the guilty bee was not one of his and 'probably a wild one' ... or at least a bit wayward.

But Luis Soltren won his case and beekeepers everywhere were reminded of their responsibilities. A more extreme reaction to a bee sting occurred in the South Devon village of Kingskerswell near Torquay in May 2011. In revenge for a single sting 18-year-old Neville Cockerham set fire to the hive and killed 54,000 bees. This rare act of mass 'apicide' earned the 'Torquay Bee Killer' a £750 fine. The sting of the law can be the most painful of all.

THE LAW IS ALL
A-TWITTER
CYBERSPACE, 2016

The first edition of *The Law's Strangest Cases* (2001) did not include the word 'twitter'. Since there were no stories about songbirds or the fussy chatter of maiden aunts it seemed superfluous. But the opening decades of the twenty-first century witnessed a profound revolution. The new age of 'social media' now renders Twitter (2006) an obligatory inclusion.

It is not alone. Myspace (2003), Facebook (2004), Flickr (2004), Bebo (2005), Tumblr (2007), Instagram (2010) and Pinterest (2011) are but a handful of the hundreds of Internet-based communication platforms used by billions the world over. Upwards of 500 million 'tweets' are posted every day. Technology has also spawned new words – *selfie, texting, sexting, googling, cyber-bullying, skype, unfriending, spam, app* – and countless more.

This new climate presents a huge challenge to the law – particularly relating to libel and defamation. The Internet has transformed our ability to communicate and access information – but it also makes it easier for us to threaten or be rude to people, to have our privacy invaded or our reputations tarnished. This has happened at breakneck speed. The law knows it must adapt – but is struggling to keep up.

The principle is long-established. The eighteenth century Lord Chief Justice William Murray noted: 'As the usages of society alter, the law must adapt itself to the various situations of mankind.' The twentieth century luminary Lord Denning oversaw many such adaptations in an age when society changed markedly. But now the pace has accelerated anew. How might Denning have reacted to a 'vexatious tweet' or the stark exposures of a 'revenge porn' case?

Denning's death in 1999 at the age of 100 marked a watershed. His was the old order – capable of progressive thinking but essentially puritanical. He once pronounced an unmarried woman who had been found with a man in her room at a teacher training college to be 'quite unsuitable for teaching.' Today's excesses might have taxed him.

There's the rub. Denning and his ilk may no longer be active, but laws framed in their time are. Courts increasingly find themselves striving to apply rules crafted in a 'former time' to today's other world of Internet surfing and social media. A Canadian judge articulated that dichotomy: 'Doggedly applying these old rules to the Internet age is like trying to fit a square archaic peg into the hexagonal hole of modernity.'

Not surprisingly the transition has delivered many unusual happenings. As *The Law's Strangest Cases* reaches its end a mere sampler must serve. Let's begin at the basic level. In April 2004 in Dauphin County, Pennsylvania, Judge Lawrence F. Clark became so irritated by a defendant's continued use of a mobile phone that he ordered a sheriff's deputy to throw it out of the fifth floor window. Clark said: 'He violated the courthouse rule. They told him not to bring that thing in here.'

Barely a year later Niagara Falls City Court Judge Robert Restaino reacted with greater wrath still. During a group hearing for domestic violence offenders in March 2005 a mobile phone began ringing. Restaino demanded to know who owned it. When nobody confessed Restaino snapped: 'Every single person in this courtroom is going to jail unless I get that instrument now.' He wasn't joking – all 46 defendants were duly detained. Only for a few hours – but it was enough to get Restaino fired after a state commission ruled he had 'deliberately and methodically violated the defendants' fundamental rights.'

These extreme reactions reflect the twitchiness of a legal world increasingly faced with the unfamiliar. Consider the UK case *The Crown v. Paul Chambers* – 'The Twitter Joke Trial'. On 10 May 2010 at Doncaster Magistrates' Court, 27-year-old trainee accountant Chambers was found guilty under the 2003 Communications Act of posting a 'menacing' tweet.

In January 2010 the closure of a South Yorkshire airport due to snow had prevented Chambers from flying to Belfast to meet a girlfriend. Venting his frustration he tweeted his 600 followers: 'Crap! Robin Hood Airport is closed. You've got a week and a bit to get your shit together otherwise I'm blowing the airport sky high.'

Although a 'joke' intended only for his own circle, the tweet came to the attention of the airport authorities, was passed to police, and an action brought. Chambers was fined £385 and ordered to pay £600 costs. He also lost his job.

Only at third appeal was the conviction quashed – on 27 July 2012 the High Court ruled 'the tweet did not constitute or include a message of a menacing character.' This landmark case placed the tricky topic of Internet 'banter' under scrutiny, and many cases since have debated 'where to draw the line online'. A curious irony of the Chambers' case was that he had met girlfriend Sarah Tonner – alias @CrazyColours – via Twitter.

A further landmark case arose in America when 18-year-old Cody Hall became the first person charged with murder as a result of his tweets. On 9 June 2013 in Dublin, California, Hall knocked down and killed 58-year-old cyclist Diana Hersevoort when driving his vehicle at 83mph (134km/h) in a 40mph (64km/h) zone. An initial charge of manslaughter was upgraded to murder after the prosecution studied Hall's Twitter feed which vividly illustrated his love of speed. Hall had boasted of driving at 140mph (225km/h) and in one tweet urged 'someone come on a death ride with me.' The prosecution held that the tweets amply demonstrated the 'implied malice' necessary to bring a murder charge.

Although Hall ultimately agreed a 'no contest' plea bargain in April 2014 to the downgraded charge of vehicular manslaughter – for which he got nine years – his 'reckless tweets' proved as much a part of the case as his 'reckless driving'. As a result lawyers everywhere warned the online community that all manner of electronic communication is increasingly considered 'admissible evidence'.

But not everybody heeds such warnings. Barely three months after Hall's conviction 27-year-old Danielle Saxton was arrested in Illinois charged with stealing a distinctive leopard-print dress from Martie's Boutique. Facebook had a double role in her capture. After the store owner posted a 'watch out for this dress' appeal, the Facebook community soon connected to Danielle, who on her own Facebook page had posted a wonderful selfie of her wearing the stolen item.

Such aberrations are surprisingly frequent – social media analysts suggest that 'impulsive posters' completely forget that the wider world is potentially looking in.

Although the United States leads the way in social media cases, the United Kingdom is closing fast. As *The Law's Strangest Cases* goes to print the number of Internet-related cases is growing apace – yet the merest tip of a huge looming iceberg has so far revealed itself.

The most progressive 'futurists' predict that technological changes over the next two decades will make those of the last 20 years seem insignificant. The virtual world will reign. One 'expert report' suggests that by 2030 many tasks currently undertaken by lawyers will be routinely done by 'robots'. A counter report concedes some automation may well occur – but 'you will still be hiring a lawyer'. Meanwhile a growing body of 'informed sceptics' suggests 'social media' is nothing but a passing fad which will eventually fade. The fact is nobody knows for sure what lies ahead – except change.

That's great news for *The Law's Strangest Cases* – it guarantees the steady supply of strangeness we have come to rely on. And amidst the as yet unimagined oddities we can only hope that some of the old standards prevail – is it too much to hope that in at least one courtroom a judge will solemnly ask the question that proves some things never change? 'What is Twitter and Facebook?'

SELECTED BIBLIOGRAPHY

Abbott, *Geoffrey. The Book of Execution*. London, Headline, 1994

Beltrami, Joseph. *The Defender. East Kilbride*, M & A Thomson, 1988

Bingham, Richard. *Modern Cases on Negligence*. London, Sweet & Maxwell, 1978

Bland, James. *True Crime Diary Volume 1*. London, Futura, 1987

Bland, James. *True Crime Diary Volume 2*. London, Macdonald, 1988

Bland, James. *Crime Strange But True*. London, Futura, 1991

Campbell, *Lord. Lives of the Chancellors*. London, Murray, 1856

Comyn, James. *Irish at Law*. London, Seeker & Warburg, 1981

Curzon, L B. *Dictionary of Law*. London, Pitman, 1996

Fido, Martin. *The Chronicle of Crime*. London, Little, Brown, 1993

Fido, Martin, & Skinner, Keith. *The Official Encyclopedia of Scotland Yard*. London, Virgin, 1999

Fleming, Justin. *Barbarism to Verdict*. Sydney, Angus & Robertson, 1994

Gaute, J.H.H., & Odell, Robin. *Murder Whatdunit*. London, Harrap, 1982

Gaute, J.H.H., & Odell, Robin. *The New Murderers' Who's Who*, London, Headline, 1989

Griffiths, Major Arthur. *Mysteries of Police and Crime*. London, Cassell, 1898

Hamilton, Dick. *Foul Bills and Dagger Money*. London, Cassell, 1979

Hooper, David. *Public Scandal, Odium and Contempt*. London, Secker & Warburg, 1984

Irving, Ronald. *The Law is a Ass*. London, Gerald Duckworth, 1999

Jones, Elwyn. *On Trial*. London, Macdonald & Jane's, 1978

Lock, Joan. *Tales from Bow Street*. London, Robert Hale,1982

Lock, Joan. *Blue Murder? Policemen Under Suspicion*. London, Robert Hale, 1986

Lustgarten, Edward. *The Judges and the Judged*. London, Odham's Press, 1961

McLynn, Frank. *Famous Trials: Cases That Made History*. London, Chancellor, 1999

Mortimer, John. *The Oxford Book of Villains*. Oxford, OUP, 1992

Pannick, David. *Judges*. Oxford, OUP, 1987

Pannick, David. *Advocates*. Oxford, OUP, 1992

Pile, Stephen. *The Book of Heroic Failures*. London, Routledge & Kegan Paul, 1979

Shaw, Karl. *The Mammoth Book of Oddballs and Eccentrics*. London, Robinson, 2000

Sparrow, Gerald. *The Great Judges*. London, John Long, 1974

Tibballs, Geoff. *Legal Blunders*. London, Robinson, 2000

Tumim, Stephen. *Great Legal Disasters*. London, Arthur Barker, 1983

Warner, Gerald. *Being of Sound Mind: Book of Eccentric Wills*. London, Elm Tree Books. 1980

Winkworth, Stephen. *More Amazing Times*. London, George Allen & Unwin, 1985

OTHER TITLES IN

THE STRANGEST® SERIES

The *Strangest* series has been delighting and enthralling readers for decades with weird, exotic, spooky and baffling tales of the absurd, ridiculous and the bizarre. This range of fascinating books – from Football to London, Rugby to Law and many subjects in between – details the very curious history of each one's funniest, oddest and most compelling characters, locations and events.

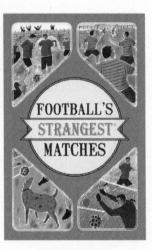

9781910232910

9781910232866

GOLF'S
STRANGEST®
ROUNDS

9781910232934

KENT'S
STRANGEST®
TALES

9781910232972

LONDON'S
STRANGEST®
TALES

9781910232880

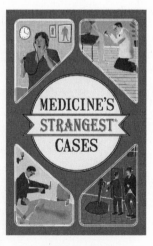

MEDICINE'S
STRANGEST®
CASES

9781910232941

MOTOR RACING'S STRANGEST RACES

9781910232965

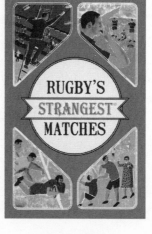

RUGBY'S STRANGEST MATCHES

9781910232873

RUNNING'S STRANGEST TALES

9781910232927

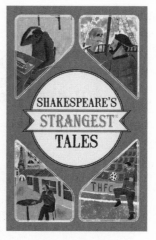

SHAKESPEARE'S STRANGEST TALES

9781910232903

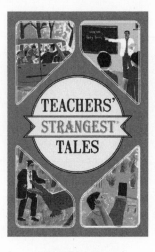

TEACHERS' STRANGEST TALES

9781910232989

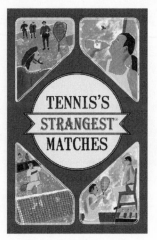

TENNIS'S STRANGEST MATCHES

9781910232958